S.LEE DAVIS

The Girl In The Window

BENT
NAIL
BOOKS

First edition

ISBN (paperback): 979-8-9986429-9-9
ISBN (hardcover): 979-8-9986429-4-4

This book was professionally typeset on Reedsy.
Find out more at reedsy.com

To every child who went unheard—
your silence was never consent.
Your survival is your rebellion.

"I tell my story
not because it is unique,
but because it is not.
It is the story of so many."

— Malala Yousafzai

Acknowledgments

To the ones who walked beside me when the road felt unbearable—
thank you. Your belief in me made the difference between silence and
voice.

To my family, both chosen and blood, who have offered love,
understanding, and space for healing—I am forever grateful.

To the brave souls who've shared their own stories with me along
the way, reminding me that we are never truly alone.

To my readers: I see you. I honor your strength, your scars, and
your journey. May this book serve as a reminder that survival is a
victory.

And to the child I once was—this is for you. You made it.

Prologue

Sarah sat in her 1999 Chevy Blazer, parked beneath a gray Kentucky sky, the engine silent. Rain slicked the windshield in steady rhythm—soft, insistent, and cleansing. The steady tap of each drop felt almost like breath against glass, like the world itself was exhaling after holding something in too long.

Across the cemetery lawn, a small procession gathered beneath umbrellas the color of coal. They moved like shadows in the downpour, blurred and slow, like the grief they carried had weight. A black casket dipped slowly into the earth, swallowed by mud and memory. Some wept. Others stared ahead blankly, lost in their own thoughts.

Sarah felt none of it.

No tears. No anger. No sadness.

Only stillness.

Only peace—profound and overdue.

She didn't join the mourners. She hadn't come to be seen. She remained parked at the edge of the cemetery, watching through the rain-smeared glass from a distance. It was how she had lived for years—on the periphery, behind invisible walls, always observing, always assessing, always surviving.

Steve was being buried today.

And she had come—not to say goodbye, not to forgive, not to mourn—but to *see*. To witness the end. To know, with her own eyes, that it was *real*. That the nightmare had a coffin now.

1

The man who had terrorized her childhood, haunted her adolescence, and cast his long, ugly shadow into the first years of her adulthood was gone. Dead. And the world somehow felt wider without him in it.

For years, she'd lived like prey—checking door locks twice, keeping her back to the wall, memorizing exits. She'd taught herself how to disappear in plain sight, how to measure her voice, how to carry herself like she didn't exist. That kind of vigilance gets into your bones. But now... now there was no one left to run from.

She rested her hands in her lap, tracing the seam of her jeans with the edge of her thumbnail. Rain tapped against the hood. The wipers squeaked softly every few seconds, wiping away a view that never really changed.

She was free.

Not long before the funeral, she had received a call from Angie—one of the few family members whose voice she could still stand to hear. Steve was in hospice. Unresponsive. Yellow with liver failure. Shrunken by years of rage and rot. Angie hadn't asked much—just thought Sarah might want to know.

She hadn't gone for him. She hadn't gone for *them*. She'd gone for *herself*.

Walking into that hospital was like stepping into the past with no flashlight. The walls smelled of antiseptic and slow death. Her feet felt heavy with every step down the hallway. Bobby met her near the door, older now, softer. His voice was quiet when he told her Steve wouldn't wake, couldn't speak, couldn't hurt her. Still, her body had screamed to turn back.

But she went in anyway.

The room was crowded with ghosts—distant cousins, weathered aunts, siblings she hadn't spoken to in years. They looked at her like nothing had ever happened. Like she was still the same girl who used to braid hair and wash dishes and keep secrets with bruised lips.

And there he was.

Steve.

The man who had stolen her childhood like a thief in the night. The man who had made her afraid to breathe too loudly, to laugh too freely, to exist in her own body. He lay motionless beneath thin hospital sheets, jaundiced, hollow-eyed, a fraction of the monster he had once been.

He looked like all the other times she'd seen him passed out— slumped in a chair or sprawled on the couch, stinking of liquor and venom. But now, there was no threat. Only a dying shell of a man who had once thrived on control.

She lasted four minutes. Maybe five.

Then the breath caught in her throat, and she fled the room.

Out in the hallway, she collapsed onto a bench, her chest shaking, her palms covering her face as the tears came—not of grief, but release. The kind of weeping that wrings something loose. That washes out rot. Bobby sat beside her, his hand on her back, saying nothing. There were no words. Only the sound of her body letting go of years.

A few days later, the call came. He was gone.

And now, she sat watching his casket disappear beneath the wet dirt, the final trace of him vanishing into the ground. There were no thunderclaps. No shrieking wind. Just the sound of rain and the low murmur of goodbye.

She thought of the girl she used to be—the one who stared out the window waiting for her mother, trying to believe that love might still come home. The one who tiptoed through silence, who kept secrets like splinters under her skin. The one who tried to make herself invisible to survive.

Now she was a woman. A mother. A survivor.

And again, she sat at a window—only this time with the storm

3

outside and peace within.

The man was dead.

The story, at long last, was hers.

And for the girl in the window—for the child who once clung to hope in the dark—

That was enough.

That was *everything*.

But peace never comes without a cost. And hers began a long time ago, in a house where nobody was watching.

I

Part One

No One Was Watching

Chapter 1

The late summer sun hung low over the rooftops, casting long amber shadows across the patchy yards of the subdivision. Cicadas had begun their evening chorus—loud and relentless—rattling the air with their song as if trying to shake loose the heat that clung to everything.

At the corner sat a small house with light pink brick and curling shingles, its yard parched and uneven. The only movement came from the tattered curtains shifting in the breeze of a window fan that clicked with every rotation, struggling to keep the thick, stale air moving.

Inside, the house felt suspended—too quiet, too still.

Cigarette smoke curled lazily near the ceiling, lingering like the words no one had the energy to say. It mingled with the scent of dish soap, sweat, and something heavier: the slow decay of uncertainty, of exhaustion, of unspoken fear. The walls themselves seemed to lean inward, like they, too, were tired of holding everything in.

Hattie stood in front of the sink, her back to the rest of the house, staring down at a basin of soapy water. A half-burned cigarette smoldered in the ashtray beside her, forgotten. The faucet hissed in contrast to the soft clinks of silverware and plates, and her hands moved mechanically—wash, rinse, stack—like muscle memory had taken over where her mind could not.

Her shoulders sagged beneath the thin halter top that clung damply to her skin. Her hair, pinned up in haste, had loosened in tendrils

7

along her neck. She looked like a woman doing dishes. But inside, she was unraveling.

John was home now, recovering—or trying to—from another heart attack. The last one had hit while he was mowing the yard in the burning afternoon sun. He'd dropped the mower handle and collapsed to his knees as Sarah watched through the window, too young to understand but old enough to know something was wrong.

Now he spent most of his time slumped in the recliner near the front window or dozing in the back bedroom, his once broad shoulders now slack beneath a sweat-stained t-shirt. His skin had gone almost translucent, and the way he moved—slow and deliberate—was like watching someone carry a weight they could no longer hide.

Sarah sat on the floor near the coffee table, her crayons spread out like spilled treasure. Her curls stuck to her forehead in sweaty spirals, her dress rumpled from a long day of waiting. She colored without focus, scribbling shapes that meant nothing, glancing up every so often toward her father's chair.

She had stopped asking when he would feel better. There hadn't been an answer the first time. Or the tenth.

Mark, older and more practiced in silence, lounged nearby with a comic book in his lap. He hadn't turned a page in nearly twenty minutes. He watched Hattie through the corner of his eye, alert for shifts—the slamming of a cabinet, the too-loud clearing of a throat, the flash in her voice that meant she was about to crack.

Nan had stayed the week before—her skin pale from the spot on her back that needed treating, her voice full of quiet warnings and soft sighs. She'd done what she could: paid some bills, made sure the kids got to bed on time, cooked real food. But she'd left the day before, retreating to Sherry's house. No one said why. But Mark knew. Nan had seen too much—the unopened mail, the empty beer cans, the way Hattie stared off at nothing for long stretches like the world had slipped just slightly out of reach.

From the recliner, John stirred, coughing hard enough to fold him forward. The sound was dry, papery, and sharp. Sarah winced.

Hattie dried her hands and walked slowly to his side. Every step looked heavier than it should have, like her body was wading through invisible water. She knelt beside him and held out a cup of water. He took it, sipped, nodded. Said nothing.

"Daddy okay?" Sarah's voice was soft, almost hopeful.

Hattie glanced back at her daughter, offered a tired smile that didn't quite reach her eyes. "He's just resting, baby. He'll feel better soon."

But something flickered across her face—something unspoken. Doubt. Resignation. Fear. Sarah didn't have a name for it, but she felt it settle in her chest like a cold stone.

That night, the house went dim with early dusk. The porch light flicked on automatically, but no one noticed. The television hummed in the background, playing a show no one was watching. A bottle clinked softly against the coffee table, then rolled onto its side. No one picked it up.

Sarah lay in bed, the box fan churning stale air beside her. From her pillow, she could hear the muffled murmur of voices in the next room. Mark's low hum of reading. The scrape of Hattie's lighter. The hollow rhythm of the recliner creaking beneath John's fragile frame.

The air outside was cooling now, the cicadas beginning to fade. But inside the house, the tension had only grown heavier, pressing into the walls like a slow-moving storm. The kind you could feel before you could see.

Sarah rolled to her side and closed her eyes tight.

Something was changing. Something in her mother's face. In her brother's quiet. In the house itself.

She didn't know what it meant yet. Only that it made her feel cold. And in the dark, she hoped—quietly, desperately—that sleep would come before the dreams did.

Chapter 2

Sarah's days had started to blend together.

With school back in session, mornings came early. The house stayed quiet in the blue-gray hush before dawn, and Sarah, just four—*almost five*—moved with practiced care, tiptoeing across cold linoleum in socked feet so she wouldn't wake her father.

She dressed herself as best she could, sometimes putting her shirt on backward or buttoning it wrong, but no one ever corrected her. She liked when the air outside bit her cheeks. It made her feel awake. Alive.

Inside, the house felt heavier.

John had been home for weeks now, still recovering from his last heart attack. He spent most of his days slumped in the recliner or asleep in bed, wrapped in an afghan that Nan had made. His skin had taken on a pale, almost grayish hue. Sometimes when Sarah passed through the room, she'd find him staring out the window like he was watching something only he could see.

He didn't talk much anymore. When he did, his voice sounded far away.

Hattie had good days and bad ones.

On good mornings, she would hum along with the radio, scramble eggs, and braid Sarah's hair so gently it made her chest ache with love. But those mornings were rare now.

Most days, she sat at the kitchen table in her robe, a cigarette burning in one hand, the long, curly phone cord twisted tight around her fingers. She'd talk low and fast to someone on the other end—usually Donna or one of the women from up the road—asking for a ride to the store or to the bar or just away. Hattie didn't drive, had never learned, so whenever she disappeared, it meant someone had come to get her.

Sarah didn't always see who.

On those days, she made herself small.

She knew the signs now—the sharpness in Hattie's voice, the way she wouldn't make eye contact, the way the empty beer cans began to gather near the sink like unwanted guests. On those mornings, Sarah dressed without help and slipped quietly out the front door with a knot in her belly and a half-buttoned coat.

Mark had grown quieter, too.

At seven, he already carried himself like someone older—like he understood things that Sarah didn't have words for yet. He checked the mail each day, glanced at the bills, watched their mother with wary eyes. When Sarah got home from school, he always asked if she'd eaten, even if all she could say was yes through a lie.

That afternoon, Sarah came home to the same stillness.

John was asleep in the recliner, the TV murmuring soft static beneath the buzz of an afternoon soap opera. Nan's afghan was pulled up to his chest. His chest rose and fell slowly, like each breath took effort. His cheeks looked sunken, and the side table beside him was scattered with pill bottles and tissues.

In the kitchen, a note sat on the counter.

"Ran to the store. Be back soon."

Hattie's handwriting, slanted and rushed.

But Sarah already knew what it meant. *The store* could mean the liquor store or Donna's house or someplace else.

Sarah couldn't read the whole note, but she recognized the words "back soon." She stood on her tiptoes and traced the loops of her mother's handwriting with a fingertip, as if the meaning might change.

She made herself a peanut butter sandwich, carefully spreading the sticky brown paste onto the bread without tearing it, just like Mark had shown her. She sat at the table, her small legs swinging above the floor, and chewed in silence.

The light from the window had already started to shift. The shadows outside grew longer, reaching toward the porch like fingers.

When she finished, she pushed her plate into the sink and tiptoed back into the living room. Her father's soft breathing and the gentle hum of the TV were the only sounds. She climbed onto the couch, curled into a tight ball, and stared out the window, resting her cheek against the cool glass.

She didn't cry. Not yet.

Instead, she let her mind wander—imagining a house where her mom was always home, where her dad could chase her through the yard again, where dinner meant plates and laughter instead of cans and silence.

The front door creaked slightly when the wind shifted. Sarah flinched but didn't move.

Eventually, Mark came home and dropped his schoolbag near the table. He nodded to Sarah, then pulled out his notebook and started his homework. He didn't ask where their mom was. He already knew.

John stirred. "Water," he croaked.

Sarah slid off the couch, padded into the kitchen, and filled a glass. She held it carefully in both hands and handed it to her father, who gave her a small nod, then dozed off again before finishing it.

The evening crept in slowly, stretching like a shadow.

It was nearly dark when Donna dropped Hattie off and the front door finally opened. Hattie breezed in with a bag of groceries and a

13

half-apology on her lips. She smelled like cigarette smoke. She smiled like she hadn't been gone for hours.

"Let's get some dinner going," she said, tousling Sarah's hair.

From the brown paper bag, she pulled out a pack of hamburger meat, a loaf of bread, a can of soup, and a carton of cigarettes. To most people, it would have looked like barely anything. But to Sarah, it felt like a feast.

Later that night, with the dishes done and the house still and dim, Sarah walked quietly to the window and pressed her fingertips to the glass. The night was dark and wide, the porch light buzzing overhead, moths flickering in and out of its glow.

She didn't know why she kept looking.

Maybe she was waiting.

Maybe she was just hoping that someday, someone might be looking back.

Chapter 3

The rain came down in a steady whisper, coating the windows in a silver sheen. The streets outside shimmered with puddles, and the gray sky pressed low as if the world itself had taken on the weight of grief.

Sarah lay curled on the couch, wrapped in a faded crocheted blanket Nan had made, the same one John had held a few days earlier. Her head throbbed with fever, and her limbs felt heavy. She'd been home sick from kindergarten that day, her cheeks flushed and skin clammy. The television murmured quietly in the background—a dull, distant voice that did little to distract her from the strange stillness in the house.

Hattie had been pacing for the last hour, restless and jittery. When the phone finally rang, Sarah lifted her head just in time to see her mother freeze in place. Hattie stared at the receiver, her hand hovering in the air for a second too long before finally picking it up.

"Hello?" she said, her voice flat.

Silence.

Then, "What?" The word cracked through the room like a whip. Hattie's other hand went to her mouth. She turned away from Sarah, but the shift in her body said everything. "Oh my God," she whispered. "Are you sure?"

Sarah sat up. "What's wrong, Momma?"

Hattie didn't answer. She hung up the phone, hands trembling. "Get your shoes on," she said quietly. "We're going to Gertie's next door. You'll stay with her for a while."

Gertie, the backyard neighbor, was kind and soft-spoken, her house always smelling like cinnamon and coffee. Sarah blinked, confused. "Why?"

"I just need you to, okay?" Hattie's voice cracked, and for the first time in a long while, she didn't sound angry—just lost.

Bill had just pulled into the driveway. Without saying more, Hattie grabbed her purse, walked Sarah through the rain to Gertie's door, and knocked. "Can you watch her?" she asked. "Just for a little bit."

Gertie took one look at her and nodded. "Of course."

Sarah stood at the window, nose pressed to the cool glass, watching as her mother climbed into Bill's car and disappeared into the storm.

She didn't know yet. Not really. She only felt it—something irreversible had happened.

Chapter 4

At the hospital, a nurse led Hattie down a sterile hallway that smelled faintly of antiseptic and loss. The fluorescent lights buzzed above her, casting cold white rectangles across the floor. Each step echoed behind her like a countdown. She wasn't ready.

The nurse opened the door with a quiet click.

"This was his room," she said gently, placing a hand on Hattie's arm.

But the bed was empty.

The blanket had already been folded back, the pillow neatly fluffed—too neat, too fast. The machines had been wheeled away. All that remained was the faint, sour scent of sweat and disinfectant and the haunting outline of where John's body had once been.

Hattie's breath caught in her throat.

She took a shaky step forward, her eyes scanning the sterile space, searching for him, needing him to still be there.

"Where is he?" she whispered.

The nurse gave her a soft look. "They moved him just a few minutes ago. I'm sorry. We didn't know you were on your way."

Hattie stood frozen at the foot of the bed. Her hand hovered in the air for a moment before she lowered herself to the mattress and sat down slowly, like the weight of the world had finally caught up with her.

Her fingers trembled as they brushed the crease in the blanket where his body had once rested.

He had been here. Right here. Moments ago. And now...

Gone.

Just like that.

She pressed her hand to her chest, trying to steady the pounding, but her heart was breaking open in real time, cracking wide with every breath. She hadn't gotten to say goodbye. Not properly. Not when it mattered.

"Why'd you leave me?" she whispered into the stillness, her voice fragile and cracking. "Why'd you leave me here to face all this alone?"

She had imagined she'd get to hold his hand one more time, to apologize for the things they never fixed, to thank him for the years they somehow managed to survive together. Instead, she was met with quiet and an empty bed.

"I wasn't ready," she said, her voice rising with a desperate edge. "John, I wasn't ready for this. For *you* to be gone. For me to be... what am I even supposed to do now?"

Her hands curled into fists in her lap as the room closed in around her. All those nights they had spent talking on porches, fighting in kitchens, falling asleep beside each other without saying a word—and now the silence was deafening.

Tears welled in her eyes but didn't fall. Not yet. She swallowed them back, the way she'd swallowed every hard thing in her life. But inside, something buckled.

A nurse returned quietly with John's wedding band in a small clear envelope.

"We thought you might want this," she said, placing it on the nightstand.

Hattie stared at it for a long time before finally reaching for it. Her fingers closed around the plastic like it was fragile, like if she wasn't careful, it might all disappear.

"I married that man when we were just kids," she murmured, more to herself than anyone. "Didn't know what the hell we were doing. But we stuck."

She wiped her cheek with the back of her hand.

"God, he was stubborn. And stupid. And mine."

The nurse gave her space.

Hattie didn't know how long she sat there—minutes, maybe hours. Time didn't make sense anymore. Nothing did. The only thing she knew for sure was that the man who had once made her laugh until her sides hurt, the man who drove her crazy and then drove her home—was gone.

And in the quiet stillness of that empty room, with nothing but memory and regret to keep her company, Hattie realized something she wasn't ready to admit, not even to herself.

She wasn't just grieving John.

She was grieving *the life they never got to finish.*

Chapter 5

The fluorescent lights in the office hummed softly above Vanessa's desk as she flipped through a thick stack of claim forms. The scent of stale coffee mixed with the faint lemon polish used on the desks, and the rhythmic clicking of her co-worker's keyboard filled the space. It was just another day at the insurance office—papers, calls, files, repeat.

She absentmindedly placed a hand on her stomach, barely swollen but still there. Her baby. She wasn't sure how to feel about it yet. Excited? Of course. Terrified? Absolutely. At 21, she was going to be a mother, but sometimes, she still felt like she had barely figured out how to be a wife.

The phone at her desk rang. She straightened up, tucking a strand of her brown hair behind her ear before picking up the receiver.

"Good afternoon, Wright & Associates. This is Vanessa speaking, how can I help you?"

It was a standard call—some elderly woman unsure if her policy covered water damage. Vanessa guided her through the fine print, her voice calm and polite, the way it always was. But as she spoke, her thoughts wandered.

She had been working here since she was eighteen. At the time, it was just supposed to be a way to help Calvin pay bills while he worked at the repair shop and did his shifts at the firehouse. But three years later, she was still here, still answering phones, still pushing paper.

A sudden flutter in her stomach made her pause. Not gas. Not hunger. Something else.

Oh.

She pressed her hand gently against her stomach, her heartbeat quickening. Had she just felt the baby move?

"Vanessa?"

She blinked. Her supervisor, Mr. Thompson, was standing at her desk, raising an eyebrow.

"Yes?" she responded, trying to shake the moment off.

"I need those Johnson files by the end of the day."

She nodded, reaching for the folder. "Of course."

But her mind was elsewhere.

—-

That evening, Vanessa walked up the steps of their small, cozy house. It wasn't much—a single-story with an aging porch and a tiny yard Calvin kept saying he'd fix up. But it was home. It was their home.

She found Calvin in the kitchen, sleeves rolled up, a screwdriver in one hand, a broken toaster in front of him. The smell of burnt wiring lingered in the air.

"You're fixing another toaster?" she teased, setting her purse down.

Calvin grinned, looking up at her with his warm brown eyes. "This one's from the firehouse. Jerry swears it can be saved."

She chuckled, walking over to press a quick kiss to his cheek. He smelled like smoke and metal, a combination of his two jobs.

"How was work?" he asked.

Vanessa hesitated. She could tell him about the endless calls, the stack of papers. But instead, she placed her hand on her stomach again, looking at him with wide eyes.

"I think I felt the baby move today."

Calvin's eyes widened, and he immediately reached out, placing his

21

rough hand over hers. They stood there in silence for a moment, both of them waiting, hoping.

Nothing.

He let out a soft chuckle. "Guess the baby's shy."

She smiled, but deep inside, there was something else. A little fear. A little sadness. She was going to be a mom. She was going to raise someone. And yet, she still felt like she barely understood what family was supposed to be.

She thought of her own parents, of the way she had learned to depend on herself because no one else would do it for her. Calvin was steady, loving, safe—but what if she wasn't enough?

"Hey," Calvin's voice was soft, drawing her back. "You okay?"

She looked at him, really looked at him, and nodded. "Yeah."

He didn't push. He never did.

Instead, he pulled her into his arms, resting his chin against her head. She closed her eyes, breathing him in, letting herself feel safe, if only for a little while.

Tomorrow, she would go back to work. Tomorrow, she would deal with her mother, her siblings, the weight of family expectations. But tonight, it was just her, Calvin, and the tiny life growing inside her.

And for now, that was enough.

Chapter 6

The night was thick with darkness when Vanessa grabbed her coat, still clutching the house phone in her other hand. The air felt unusually still, like the world had paused just long enough for her to feel the weight of whatever was coming.

"Should I drive you?"

She turned toward her husband, strands of her short brown hair falling across her forehead. She brushed them away with a shaky breath, locking eyes with Calvin. His face was laced with concern.

"No, no... it's okay," she murmured.

"You sure, honey?" His voice was gentle but firm.

Vanessa nodded, though her entire body felt like it was humming just beneath the surface. Her eyes wavered, unable to fully meet his. She put the phone back on its cradle and forced a small, unconvincing smile.

"It's fine, Calvin. I'll be back soon."

At least, she hoped she would. She prayed that Mom's shaky voice calling her so late wasn't for something terrible. But deep down, the dread had already bloomed in her gut and taken root.

She slipped into her coat and hurried out the door. The wind bit at her cheeks as she moved, but she barely felt it. Once in the car, she gripped the steering wheel tightly, white-knuckled, and backed out of the driveway into the inky blackness of the neighborhood.

The drive was short—five, maybe ten minutes—but it felt like an eternity. The streetlights cast long shadows that stretched across the cracked pavement. Familiar intersections suddenly felt foreign. Her chest tightened with each turn, and the headlights on the empty road seemed too bright, too quiet, like the world was holding its breath.

When she pulled into the familiar driveway, the house looked… still. Not dark, not lit. Just still.

She sat in the car for a moment, staring at the back porch light glowing faintly through the kitchen curtains. Then something made her glance toward the rear of the house. A sliver of movement through the side window—shadows passing, lights flickering.

Instead of going to the front door, Vanessa walked around the side of the house and stepped quietly onto the back stoop. The kitchen door opened with a creak, and she slipped inside.

The smell of smoke hit her first—cigarettes and something older, stale, like something had been slowly burning out for a long time. The house was quiet except for the distant hum of a television somewhere down the hall. She peeled off her coat and draped it over the nearest chair.

"Vanessa?"

The voice was soft, fragile. When she turned, Hattie was standing by the kitchen table, her cigarette burning low in the ashtray beside her, a smudge of ash trailing across the Formica surface. She looked… diminished. Her shoulders curled inward like she was trying to hold herself together.

"Mom…" Vanessa stepped forward. "What's going on? What happened?"

She reached out, placing a hand gently on Hattie's arm. The contact made her mother flinch.

"I…" Hattie started, then stopped. Her lips moved, but no words came. Her eyes darted away.

"Mom," Vanessa said again, firmer this time. "Tell me."

Hattie stood abruptly, wiping her hands down the sides of her jeans even though they weren't dirty. "No, no, sit down," she said, a strange tremble in her voice. "I—I need to get Randy first."

Vanessa blinked. "Wait, what? What's happening?"

But Hattie was already halfway down the hallway.

Vanessa stayed frozen, the silence pressing against her chest. The weight in the air was suffocating.

A minute later, she heard the low thud of footsteps. Then Randy appeared in the hallway behind their mother, rubbing sleep from his eyes. He looked confused, the lines of sleep still on his face.

"What's going on?" he asked groggily, his voice cracking.

Hattie didn't answer. She moved into the living room like a ghost, settling herself onto the edge of the couch. She looked at them both—Vanessa standing, Randy hovering by the armchair—and for a long moment, she didn't speak.

Then she opened her mouth, and her voice cracked in half.

"He's gone," she said.

The words hung in the air like smoke. Heavy. Slow. Sinking.

Vanessa's eyes blinked in disbelief. "What?"

"Your dad," Hattie whispered. "He died this afternoon."

Randy took a step backward, like the words had physically struck him. "No..."

"I was at the hospital," Hattie went on, her voice shaking. "They called and said he was gone before I got there. He'd been getting weaker, but I didn't think... I didn't think it would be this fast."

Vanessa's hands flew to her mouth. She let out a small sound—half sob, half gasp—and sank into the nearest chair.

"I didn't get to say goodbye," Hattie said, her voice suddenly small, like a child's. "He was just... gone. By the time I got there, the bed was empty."

For a moment, no one spoke. The room was filled only with the loud hum of the refrigerator and the soft roar of something on the TV in another room.

Randy stepped forward, then stopped. His face was pale, stunned. "Does Mark know? Does Sarah?"

Hattie shook her head slowly. "Not yet. Mrk was at school when the hospital called. I took Sarah next door to Gertie's. I didn't want her to see me like this. I didn't know what to do."

Vanessa stood and moved toward her brother. She wrapped her arms around him and pulled him close. He didn't resist. He folded into her like he had when he was small, when he was scared of thunderstorms or nightmares.

And maybe this was both.

A storm and a nightmare.

"I should've been there," Randy said into her shoulder. "I should've been there for him."

"There was nothing you could've done," Hattie said. "It happened so fast."

Vanessa's eyes were wet now. Her voice thick. "What are we going to do?"

"I don't know," Hattie whispered. "I don't know anything right now."

But the silence that followed said everything.

The house, once full of a thousand familiar sounds—John's laugh, his footsteps, the way he'd jingle the change in his pockets when he walked through the door—suddenly felt hollow.

And in that moment, something shifted in all of them. A line had been drawn. There was life before this night—and now, everything that would come after.

Chapter 7

"Hiya, Brandy!"

Brandy squinted against the fading sunlight, her dark blue eyes narrowing at the small figure waving from the next porch over. Kirsten—her teenage neighbor—was bouncing barefoot on the cracked concrete, a tattered cardboard sign in one hand and an empty plastic donation bucket in the other.

"I don't have any change, Kirsten," Brandy called, jamming her key into the door lock.

"Old clothes will do just fine! It's for charity!"

Brandy sighed, the heat of the day still clinging to her skin like a second layer of exhaustion. She twisted the key hard and shouldered open the door. "Not tonight, kid."

She stepped inside and shut the door firmly behind her.

The apartment exhaled around her, cooler than the thick L.A. heat outside but stale, still. She kicked off her shoes and tossed her bag to the floor, stretching out her legs with a low groan. Her joints ached. Her feet throbbed. Another long shift behind her.

"Another day in Burbank," she muttered.

The words didn't hold much feeling—just a mix of weariness and numb survival.

Her dark hair had fallen loose from its clip, strands sticking to the sweat along her temple. She brushed them back, walking slowly into the kitchen. It was small, barely big enough for two people to stand in, and held the scent of canned soup and overworked air conditioning.

Freedom, she reminded herself. Cramped, quiet, lonely—but hers.

She had worked too hard for this apartment, for the right to be left alone. She didn't miss Kentucky, not really. Not the eyes watching her every move. Not the house with too many ghosts and too little comfort.

She was halfway through unbuttoning her blouse when the phone rang.

Brandy paused, head tilted.

Nobody called her landline. She barely used it herself. She hesitated, glanced at the clock—5:07 p.m.—then shook her head and turned back toward the groceries on the floor.

The phone rang again.

Her stomach fluttered.

Something about it felt wrong. Off.

She crossed the room in three strides and picked up the receiver. "Hello?"

There was a pause. Just long enough to draw breath.

Then: "Brandy…"

She froze.

That voice. Unmistakable. Weary. Fragile.

"…Mom?"

Her grip on the phone tightened.

This can't be good.

"What is it?" she asked, a bit too sharply, her voice suddenly taut with tension.

"I—I'm calling to talk, Brandy. It's really important."

Her mother never called just to talk. Not in years. Not unless something had gone wrong.

Brandy swallowed. Her heart thudded painfully against her ribs.

"What is it, Mom?" she asked again, her tone quieter now.

There was a shaky breath on the other end. Then the words came, splintered and soft.

"Honey, I don't know how to tell you this, and I hate saying it over the phone..."

Brandy already knew. Her stomach dropped.

No.

Please, no.

"It's your father," Hattie whispered. "He... he died this afternoon at the hospital."

Silence.

The kind of silence that's loud with disbelief. Brandy didn't speak. Couldn't.

The words hit her like a body blow. Her vision blurred as heat surged behind her eyes, and suddenly her knees felt weak.

Dead?

That wasn't possible. He had been sick, yes. But this? Now?

A sob clawed its way up her throat. She turned away from the kitchen, collapsing onto the edge of her couch, the phone still clutched tight in her hand.

"I... I didn't know," she whispered. "I thought he just needed to eat better. They said he could bounce back if he tried—" Her voice cracked. "I thought we had more time."

"I did too," Hattie choked. "It happened so fast. One minute they were adjusting his oxygen, and the next..." Her voice broke. "They said they just couldn't get him back this time"

Brandy leaned over, pressed the heel of her hand to her forehead, tears rolling hot down her cheeks.

"God, I wasn't ready for this."

"I don't know what to do," Hattie said. "Everything's happening so fast. I feel like I can't breathe."

There was a long pause between them.

Brandy wiped her face roughly, pulling in a ragged breath. "When's the funeral?"

"I don't know yet. I'll figure it out tomorrow. When can you come?"

Brandy didn't hesitate.

"I'll be on the first plane in the morning."

Her mother went quiet on the other end of the line. Brandy could hear her sniffling, her breath shaking.

"I'll see you tomorrow then," Hattie said, her voice small. "I love you."

Brandy's throat tightened.

"...I love you too, Mom."

She hung up.

And for the first time in years—after everything, after all the running, after all the anger—Brandy cried. Not just for the man she'd lost. But for all the versions of him they'd never gotten to know again.

For all the things left unsaid.

For the girl in her who had just lost her father.

Chapter 8

Brandy stared at the open suitcase on her bed, her mind as scattered as the half-folded clothes inside. Her apartment, usually her haven of silence and distance, felt smaller than usual—its walls pressing in, thick with memories she'd kept at bay for years.

She was flying back to Kentucky in a few hours.

Home.

The word lingered like something sour in her mouth. She hadn't called it that in a long time—not since she'd packed her life into two duffel bags and boarded a Greyhound west. Not since she stopped believing that family meant safety.

Now, she had no choice but to go back.

She sat on the edge of the bed, running a hand through her tangled hair. The suitcase gaped open in front of her, half-stuffed with clothes she barely remembered folding. Packing should've been simple—just three days, maybe four. But every shirt, every pair of jeans felt like a decision too heavy for her hands.

Her father was gone.

Just like that.

The man who'd once towered over her like a god, who could crush her with a single word, was now gone. The weight of it hit her in bursts—sharp and searing, then numb. She had spent years building walls he couldn't climb, convincing herself she didn't care.

But now there was no fixing anything. No phone call. No letter. No chance.

She clenched a blouse in her fists, her jaw tightening. What would she have even said if she'd had the time?

Why couldn't you understand me?

Why didn't you fight harder?

Why didn't you love me better?

She didn't know. And now she never would.

A knock at the door pulled her from the spiral.

Brandy frowned, glancing at the clock—11:48 p.m.

Who the hell...?

Dragging herself up, she shuffled barefoot across the cold tile and peered through the peephole.

Of course.

Kirsten.

She opened the door just enough to let her irritation breathe. "What?"

Kirsten beamed like a streetlight. "Hey! Since you're going out of town, I thought maybe I could borrow some stuff? Just a few things you won't be using."

Brandy blinked. The audacity of this girl was a whole personality trait.

"My dad just died, Kirsten." Her voice was flat. Hollow.

Kirsten's smile wobbled. "Oh. Right. Sorry." She paused, then tilted her head. "But... I mean, you're still leaving, right?"

Brandy didn't answer. Not with words. She just stared at her—long enough to drain the color from Kirsten's face—then shut the door.

Click.

Leaning against the wood, she let out a slow exhale, her breath fogging the brass deadbolt. This town was unhinged.

She made her way back to the bed, barely glancing at the half-packed suitcase before collapsing beneath the blanket. The sheets were cool against her skin, but her thoughts burned.

Sleep did not come.

Her body stayed still, but her mind traveled—back to the hollering arguments, the slammed doors, the sting of being called "too much" and "never enough" in the same breath. She thought of the last time she saw him, the way he looked at her like she was a stranger. The years she'd spent telling herself that was fine.

But now?

Now there was only silence.

Brandy turned onto her side, staring at the wall as her chest tightened with something sharp and unshakable.

Was he disappointed in me all the way to the end?

She didn't cry again. Not yet.

But she blinked, and tears gathered anyway—uninvited, quiet, heavy.

She would never know what he'd been thinking in his final moments. Never know if he regretted the distance. Never know if he forgave her for leaving—or if he thought she'd never come back at all.

And that uncertainty, more than anything, was what kept her awake long after the suitcase had been zipped.

Long after the apartment went still.

Long after the chance for any last words had disappeared with the man who could no longer give them.

Chapter 9

"Sarah! There's one more bowl of cereal left, and if you don't get here fast, I'm gonna finish it!"

Mark's voice echoed through the hallway, playful and taunting.

Sarah shot out of the bathroom, foam still clinging to the corners of her mouth. Her legs were a little shaky—she was just getting over a stomach bug—but she was faster than she'd been the day before. Faster than the day she could barely lift her head.

Mark was already at the table, tilting the cereal box over his bowl with a smirk when Sarah lunged forward and yanked it from his hands.

"Mark!" she huffed, clutching the box to her chest.

"You were taking too long," he said with a shrug, unfazed.

"It's not yours!"

She poured the cereal into her bowl with dramatic urgency, sloshing in the milk like it was a race. It was her first real meal in a day, and every crunchy bite felt like victory.

But then she saw her.

Hattie sat at the kitchen table, bathed in soft sunlight that poured through the window, but there was no warmth in her face. One hand rested limply in her lap, the other on a cup of coffee. Her shoulders sagged, and her eyes stared through the glass like she wasn't really there.

Sarah stilled, spoon halfway to her mouth.

Mark noticed it too. The smirk faded from his face. He pulled at the loose threads on his sleeve, his eyes flicking from their mother to Sarah and back again.

Something felt wrong.

Neither of them said it out loud.

When they finished eating, they told Hattie they were going outside. She didn't look at them. She barely nodded.

The air outside was warm, scented with damp grass and lingering summer heat. Cicadas buzzed from the trees, and the pavement radiated a gentle heat through the soles of Sarah's shoes. She bounced on her toes, grateful to feel well enough to run again.

"What should we do?" she asked, looking to Mark for an idea.

But before he could answer, they noticed the two figures watching them from across the street.

Roy and Kim stood on their front porch, whispering behind their hands. Their eyes didn't sparkle with mischief or laughter. They weren't inviting anyone over to play tag.

They were staring.

Mark's hand found Sarah's and held it tight.

"Let's go find Josh and Amy," he muttered. "We can play treasure hunt."

But before they could turn, Roy called out.

"Hey, Mark!"

They stopped.

Mark turned slowly. "What?"

"You're acting weird today," Roy said.

Mark frowned. "What do you mean?"

Kim stepped forward, her voice louder than a whisper should have been. "If our dad died, we wouldn't be out here playing like nothing happened."

The words dropped like a bomb.

Sarah felt her whole body freeze. Her fingers gripped Mark's shirt.

"What did you say?" Mark asked, his voice suddenly small.

Roy shrugged. "Your dad. He died. Our dad took your mom to the hospital yesterday. Didn't she tell you?"

Mark's mouth opened, but no words came.

Kim nodded. "He went to heaven. That's what my daddy said."

Mark shook his head. "No. He's sick. That's all."

Sarah's voice cracked as she tugged at his arm. "Mark? What are they talking about? Daddy's not dead... is he?"

"Don't listen to them," Mark muttered, pulling her away. "They don't know what they're saying."

But his hand trembled in hers.

"Mark, what does dead mean?" she asked, stumbling beside him.

He didn't answer.

"Mark..."

He stopped walking. His back to her. His shoulders trembling.

"It means..." He paused, choking on the words. "It means we won't see him anymore."

Her small face scrunched with confusion. "See who?"

But deep down, she already knew.

They crossed the yard quickly now, the air thicker, heavier. The warmth of the sun couldn't reach them anymore.

Inside, their mother still sat at the kitchen table.

She hadn't moved.

Mark let go of Sarah's hand and stepped forward.

"Is it true?" he asked, his voice cracking. "Is Dad really dead?"

Hattie turned her head slowly, like every muscle resisted the motion. Her eyes, blue and glassy, met his.

"Yes," she said softly.

Mark staggered back as if struck.

"Why didn't you tell us?" His voice rose. "Why didn't you just say it?"

"I was going to," Hattie whispered. "I just... I didn't know how."

Sarah stood frozen. "Mommy?"

Hattie turned to her, her expression broken.

"Where's Daddy?" Sarah asked, her voice thin as paper.

Hattie knelt in front of her and cupped her cheeks in both hands.

"Sweetheart," she said, "Daddy's in heaven now."

Sarah blinked. "Can I see him?"

Hattie swallowed hard. "No, baby. I'm sorry. You can't."

"Why not?"

"Because... he has to stay with God now."

Sarah's bottom lip quivered.

"But I want him here," she whispered.

"I know," Hattie breathed. "I know."

Behind them, Mark stood in the doorway, silent and shaking. His fists were clenched at his sides.

And that was the moment everything changed.

The house, once filled with his laughter, now echoed with silence. The walls knew something the children couldn't name yet. The air carried a weight it hadn't before.

John Dawson was gone.

And though none of them fully understood it yet, they felt it in their bones—that life would never go back to the way it had been.

Not ever again.

Chapter 10

The day after John's death passed in a fog so thick it seemed to cling to the walls, seeping into the baseboards and softening the light that filtered through the kitchen window. The house moved on without him, but nothing inside it did. It was as if time had buckled and spilled across the floor, uncontained and aimless.

Everyone drifted through the rooms like ghosts, their footsteps muffled by grief. Doors opened and closed. Water boiled. The refrigerator hummed. But no one spoke of the thing they were now orbiting—his absence.

Vanessa sat curled on the end of the couch, the receiver wedged between her shoulder and ear as she flipped through the stained pages of the yellow pages. Her voice was steady, too steady, as she read names aloud and jotted down notes on a yellow legal pad. She'd cried herself hoarse the night before, but now her grief had folded inward, contained behind the practiced rhythm of phone calls and funeral planning.

At the kitchen table, Hattie sat motionless. A cigarette burned low between her fingers, its ash growing long and unsteady. The coffee in front of her had gone cold hours ago. Smoke spiraled into the air above her, twisting like the thoughts she couldn't voice. Her face was a dull mask—blank, unreadable, eerily calm.

Randy hadn't spoken more than ten words since the night before.

He wore a shadow across his face that hadn't been there yesterday. He paced the porch in silence, his hands shoved deep into his pockets, his jaw clenched so tight the muscles in his face twitched. Every few minutes, he'd stop and rake a hand through his hair, then start pacing again—like if he stood still too long, he might fall apart. There was a restlessness in his movements, like he was trying to outrun the weight sitting heavy on his chest.

Brandy was flying in the next morning.

The house itself felt unrecognizable, like it had changed overnight—grown darker somehow, more brittle. Even the wallpaper, once bright with its faded yellow roses, now looked foreign, as though it belonged to someone else's story.

Sarah wandered from room to room, her eyes scanning for something she couldn't name. She paused often at the window, her small hand pressed to the glass, her breath fogging the pane. She kept waiting to hear the jangle of coins in her father's pocket, to see him walking up the sidewalk, his shirt damp from work, calling her his little shadow.

But the sidewalk stayed empty.

And the door never opened.

Mark, too, was quieter than usual. Not the way he got when he was annoyed or thinking, but a stillness that made him seem older than seven. He sat cross-legged on the floor, his coin collection spread around him like a ritual. But he didn't sort them. He just shifted them from one spot to another, as if waiting for them to mean something again.

When Hattie finally opened a can of green beans and made toast for dinner, no one said a word. Sarah poked at the soggy toast until it went cold. She didn't want it, not really. Her mouth felt full of sawdust. Eventually, Mark took her plate without a word and scraped it into the trash.

The silence was thicker than the smoke in the kitchen.

That night, long after the lights dimmed and the house had settled into its uneasy hush, Sarah crept down the hallway, barefoot and silent. The living room was washed in soft yellow light from the streetlamp outside. It bled through the blinds in long, crooked stripes across the floor.

John's recliner sat in its usual spot, angled just slightly toward the television, like it had always been. But the man who used to occupy it—the one who filled it with warmth and movement—was gone.

Sarah dropped to her knees beside it. She leaned her head against the armrest, and the scent of Old Spice, tobacco, and engine oil clung faintly to the fabric. The tears came suddenly, flooding over her before she could stop them. Her small shoulders heaved with quiet sobs.

She didn't cry loudly. She didn't want to wake anyone. But the silence around her made each breath sound like thunder in her chest.

She didn't hear Mark until he sat down beside her, his knees brushing hers.

He didn't say anything. He didn't have to.

He just leaned into her—solid, familiar—and together they sat on the carpet, surrounded by the hush of absence. The air between them filled with all the things they couldn't say, with the weight of what they both now knew: their father was really gone.

The next morning, Mark was the one who made the call. Vanessa looked up in surprise as he picked up the phone and dialed Randy's work number.

"He needs to come home," Mark said simply, then hung up.

When Randy arrived that evening, he looked different. His face was drawn, his eyes sunken with exhaustion that sleep couldn't fix. He stepped inside and wrapped his arms around Vanessa, like the weight of it all had finally become too much to carry alone.

Sarah ran to him the second she saw him.

She didn't say a word. Just clung to him with everything she had.

He picked her up without hesitation and held her close, his voice a breath in her hair.

"It's okay."

Even though it wasn't.

That night, the siblings gathered in the living room.

Vanessa. Randy. Mark. Sarah.

They left a space on the couch for Brandy.

Sarah curled beside Randy, her cheek resting on his arm as she listened.

Vanessa cleared her throat. "We need to decide," she said, her voice calm but tight. "About the service. The flowers. Who's going to speak."

Hattie didn't answer. She stared at the floor, her cigarette burning to the filter. Finally, she shook her head.

"I can't do this," she whispered.

"You don't have to do it alone," Randy said gently. "We'll help."

But Hattie stood and walked out of the room without looking back.

Randy leaned into the recliner—John's recliner—his hand covering his face.

"She's not going to make it through this," he muttered.

Vanessa crossed her arms. "She doesn't have a choice."

Sarah looked at them both. Their voices were lower, heavier. Different. Like they had all aged ten years in two days.

She closed her eyes and leaned harder into Randy's side.

The house didn't echo with her father's footsteps anymore. The man who had once made everything steady was gone.

And in the quiet that followed, even the walls seemed to grieve.

Chapter 11

Two days later, John Dawson's death hung over the house like humidity before a storm—thick, inescapable, and suffocating. The air felt too still, like even the breeze didn't dare pass through the open windows.

Vanessa came by early to help with the things no one wanted to do—phone calls, dishes, arrangements, silence. She would also be driving Hattie to the airport later that day to pick up Brandy, who was flying in from California. The living room was unnaturally quiet, Hattie's voice thin and drifting whenever she spoke at all, which wasn't often. The phone sat off the hook for long stretches of time. Even the television stayed off, as if no one could bear to hear anything louder than a whisper.

Down the hall, the door to Randy's room was closed.

Inside, he lay sprawled across his unmade bed, one arm hanging off the side, fingertips brushing against the cool chrome of the motorcycle he'd spent three years building. It took up half the room, its frame crouched like a beast waiting to run, the engine quiet but alive. The scent of grease, metal, and old denim filled the air, cut only by the faint crackle of a record spinning on the dresser—grainy rock, worn soft with overplay, Lynyrd Skynyrd, the needle dragging across the vinyl like a heartbeat too tired to keep rhythm.

The room looked like it had given up too—wrinkled jeans slung over a cracked chair, a high school diploma face-down on the floor, old cleats still caked with dried mud by the door. Manuals and magazines were stacked in leaning towers against the walls, while a single photograph of him and his father fishing on the Ohio River had slid halfway out of its frame and leaned awkwardly in the corner, as if it, too, had lost its footing.

Randy sat up slowly, the weight of grief still fresh in his chest, pressing in like a vise. He reached for the socket wrench on the windowsill and turned toward the bike—the only thing that made sense anymore. He tightened a bolt with practiced ease, not because it was loose, but because it gave his hands something to do.

He remembered the way his father had stood over him in the garage, offering guidance without criticism. "You gotta listen to the machine, son," John used to say. "It'll tell you what it needs. Just like people will, if you're payin' attention."

Randy swallowed hard, the echo of that voice nearly undoing him.

A knock came at the door, soft but certain.

"Randy?" It was Vanessa.

He hesitated before answering. "Yeah."

The door creaked open, and she stepped inside carefully, avoiding the clutter with practiced grace. She was dressed in a soft ivory sweater stretched slightly at the belly, her denim bell-bottoms skimming across the worn carpet. The light caught her eyes—so much like their mother's, but steadier.

The room smelled like oil, stale pizza, and unspoken things.

"I just wanted to check on you," she said gently. "You've been in here all day."

Randy didn't look up. "I'm fine."

She crossed her arms. "Liar."

He finally met her gaze, a tired smile tugging at one corner of his mouth. "You always could call bullshit better than anyone."

Vanessa walked over and perched on the edge of the bed, brushing her hand over the twisted sheet beside her. "You've been thinking about Dad."

He didn't need to answer. She could see it in the slump of his shoulders, the wrench clutched in his hand like a lifeline.

"I keep thinking," he finally said, "if I'd been around more. Maybe I could've noticed something. Maybe I could've done something."

Vanessa reached out and took his hand, her grip sure and warm. "You were working. You were living your life. You didn't do anything wrong."

He blinked hard. "But I wasn't here."

"None of us were," she said softly. "And he wouldn't want you to carry this."

Randy looked down at their hands. "I just... I miss him."

"I do too." Her voice cracked, but she kept her grip steady. "More than I can say."

They sat together in the quiet. For a moment, neither of them spoke. The needle on the record reached the end of the song and clicked softly in place, a reminder that even music eventually runs out.

Randy exhaled slowly, then tried for levity. "You're gettin' all sentimental on me. Must be the hormones."

Vanessa rolled her eyes and nudged his shoulder. "Or maybe I just know my little brother better than he thinks."

He chuckled, the sound raw but real.

She stood, smoothing her sweater. "Come by tomorrow. Calvin's grilling pork chops. You know how bad he is at not burning them."

Randy gave a small nod. "Yeah. Maybe."

Vanessa lingered in the doorway. "We'll be expecting you."

After she left, the door clicked shut behind her, and the room was still again.

But it didn't feel so heavy this time. Just quiet. Just waiting.

Randy looked back at the bike, the one thing that had always made him feel close to something real. He didn't know exactly what came next, but he knew what he wanted.

He wanted to build something.

He wanted to carry what his father had given him forward—not just the tools or the knowledge, but the love buried beneath the grit and calluses.

He leaned forward, gripped the wrench again, and got back to work.

Outside, the sky was turning the dusky blue of early evening. And inside, in the room that smelled like metal and memory, the boy John Dawson had raised was still listening—still fixing.

Still holding on.

Chapter 12

The house was quiet in the way only grief could make it—deep, echoing, oppressive. Even the air seemed to tiptoe through the halls, afraid to disturb the silence. Hattie sat on the edge of her bed, the dim glow of the bedside lamp throwing long shadows across the room. Her hands lay motionless in her lap. Her eyes, dry now, had given up trying to cry. The tears would come again. But for the moment, she was hollow.

She leaned back slowly, her spine stiff, her muscles aching in a way that went deeper than bone. She closed her eyes.

And slipped backward—years and years—into memory.

She had been eighteen. A girl with a bad home perm, a drawer full of handmade dresses, and a heart full of restless wanting. That's when she met John Dawson. He'd walked into the diner one night with a couple of rowdy boys from Eastern High School, letterman jackets and big voices. But John wasn't like the others. He had a quiet confidence, a crooked smile, and eyes that stayed on hers longer than they should have.

He had ordered black coffee and a slice of cherry pie. Stayed until closing. Talked about the Air Force like it was a ticket to someplace better. She had stood there behind the counter, the smell of burnt fries clinging to her apron, pretending she didn't notice the way her heart fluttered every time he smiled.

They didn't fall in love—they ran toward it like it was the only way out of a burning house.

By spring, they were married.

It wasn't a church wedding, not the kind she'd dreamed about as a little girl. There were no flowers, no cake, no music. Just a courthouse in Jeffersontown, a bored judge with a cold cup of coffee, and the trembling promise of something bigger than either of them knew how to hold. Her dress was pale blue cotton, stitched by hand on Nan's sewing machine. He wore slacks that didn't quite fit and a white button-down that smelled faintly of motor oil.

They said their vows like a secret, both too young to know how hard keeping it would be.

Their honeymoon was a two-night stay in a creaky one-room cabin in Gatlinburg. The fireplace smoked. The water pressure was terrible. But the mountains wrapped around them like a quilt. They drank too much Coke, laughed too loud in public, and kissed like time didn't matter.

He held her hand everywhere they went. She remembered that most of all.

But then he left.

Basic training pulled him to San Antonio. And Hattie returned to the soft defeat of her parents' house, where the air always smelled like Pabst Blue Ribbon and regret. She wrote to John every night, pouring the days into long, careful letters—what she'd cooked, how the garden was growing, which customers had tipped well and which hadn't. She'd press them to her chest before dropping them in the mailbox, like maybe he could feel her through the paper.

His replies were short. Tired. Rushed. But the moment his handwriting appeared on the envelope, she forgave the brevity.

Weeks later, the nausea started.

She blamed the eggs at first. Then the nerves. But deep down, she knew.

The clinic confirmed it. She was barely nineteen, barely out of girlhood, and already someone's mother.

She remembered the ache in her chest as she sat on her childhood bed, staring at the wall, one hand resting lightly over her stomach. She had never felt so alone—or so sure of something. The letter she wrote to John that night took two hours to finish.

"John, there's something I need to tell you..."

He called as soon as the letter reached him.

"You're pregnant?" His voice had cracked with disbelief, then bloomed with laughter—big, boyish, reckless laughter that wrapped around her like sunlight. "We're gonna have a baby?"

She cried. Not because she was scared, though she was. But because in that moment, she wasn't alone anymore. Not really.

And now...

Now the house was still. The man who had held her hand through so many messy years was gone. And she was sitting on their bed in a nightgown that no longer fit right, staring at nothing, listening to the house creak around her like an old ship that had lost its anchor.

Her hand drifted to the nightstand, where a shoebox of memories sat just beneath the drawer. She opened it slowly. Inside were snapshots from their earliest days: John in uniform, laughing in the doorway of their first apartment; a Polaroid from Gatlinburg, his arm slung around her shoulder, her smile unguarded and wide.

She picked that one up, held it close, and ran her thumb over his face. The photo had started to fade at the corners, just like everything else.

"I miss you," she whispered, her voice frayed thin.

The air didn't answer.

But something stirred in her chest, like the ghost of that old warmth. Like the echo of his laugh in the back of her mind.

She sat there for a long time, the photograph pressed to her heart, rocking gently like a mother calming herself. And for the first time since the hospital, the tears came—not sharp and frantic, but slow and steady.

They didn't wash the grief away.

But they made space for it.

Chapter 13

The funeral home smelled like grief disguised as beauty—lilies, carnations, and roses packed tightly into ornate sprays, their perfume so thick it choked the air. Sweetness gone sour. It clung to everything: the velvet upholstery, the hems of black dresses, the breath in everyone's lungs. The flowers tried to soften the blow of death, but all they did was make the room feel like a coffin dressed up for company.

The people gathered looked like shadows of themselves—dull, pale, broken in different ways. They murmured in hushed tones, dabbing their eyes, trading stories about John Dawson like he was already a memory. A man they had loved. A man who had once been the sun around which a little family spun.

"He'd give you the shirt off his back."

"Always showed up. Rain or shine."

"Good man. Steady. The kind this world don't make anymore."

Sarah stood in the center of it all, too small for the suit dress she wore, too young to understand why it all sounded like a goodbye she hadn't agreed to. She hated every word.

Mark held her hand, his grip too tight, his jaw locked. He didn't blink much anymore. Not even at this. Seven years old, and already something inside him had turned to stone.

"We've got to depend on each other now," he whispered, his voice quiet but certain. "As long as we stick together, we'll be okay."

Sarah frowned. "What about Mommy?"

Mark looked away. "She'll still be here... but I think we're gonna have to look out for ourselves now. She's got a lot to carry."

Even at four, Sarah understood what he meant. Without Dad, everything had come unmoored. Her mother drifted through the house like a ghost, present but unreachable. It was Dad who had made them feel safe. Dad who made things work.

"There you are."

Vanessa's voice, soft and strained, cut through the thick quiet. She appeared like an anchor in a storm—her light brown hair pulled back, her face blotchy from crying. But her arms opened, and Sarah ran to them like a lifeline.

"Vannie," she breathed, pressing her face into her sister's coat.

Vanessa knelt, hugging her close, one hand cradling the back of her head. "Hey, kiddo."

When she pulled away, her gaze shifted to Mark—something more than sympathy in her eyes. Something like sorrow layered with worry. Behind her, Calvin stood rigid in his funeral clothes, eyes darting around like he wasn't sure where to look or how to breathe in a room this heavy.

Vanessa guided them into the main room where the service would begin. There was no casket. No procession. Just a small wooden urn, polished to a shine, sitting on a velvet-draped table. Too quiet. Too still. Sarah stared at it, the twist in her belly growing tighter.

Was that really all that was left of her father? That little box?

No warm hand to hold. No chance to say goodbye. Just a cold statement—He's gone—and an urn in a room that smelled like flowers trying to lie.

She wanted more. A grave. A stone. Something she could touch and talk to. But all she had was that box. And the silence that followed it.

The days that came next lost their names.

Sarah spent long hours in her room, staring at the ceiling, tracing the cracks in the plaster like they might tell her how to feel. Outside the door, life moved on in whispers. The clatter of dishes. The static hum of the TV. Mark's voice—once loud and playful—muted now, as if he too was afraid to take up space.

Hattie barely emerged. When she did, she floated like smoke, her beer bottle a permanent fixture in her hand. She didn't ask about school. She didn't notice when they ate or if they were dressed. She didn't speak unless spoken to. And even then, her voice came from somewhere far away.

Randy tried to fill in the gaps. He made meals, simple ones. He set alarm clocks. He checked homework. But the way his shoulders hunched, the way he stared at the floor like it might open up and swallow him, betrayed just how hard he was holding everything together.

One morning, as he helped Sarah into her coat, she looked up at him with big, unsure eyes.

"Is Mom okay?"

He paused, fingers frozen over the zipper. "Yeah," he said, not meeting her gaze. "She just... misses Dad."

"I miss Dad too," Sarah whispered.

Randy's breath hitched. "Yeah, kid. We all do."

But Hattie wasn't just sad. She was disappearing.

At first, it was quiet. She stopped cooking. Stopped doing laundry. Stopped asking questions. Then she stopped leaving her bedroom.

Some nights, Sarah would peek into the hallway and see a thin strip of light under Hattie's door. Other nights, not even that. The house felt heavier when she was home, like her grief had a gravity all its own.

One night, Sarah tiptoed into the kitchen to get a drink and found Hattie standing in front of the open fridge, her face pale in the yellow glow. She just stood there, staring at the rows of ketchup bottles and beer cans like they might suddenly offer answers. She didn't even notice Sarah watching.

Vanessa saw it too. She came by often, trying to help—cleaning the kitchen, folding laundry, checking in on Mark and Sarah. But even she was starting to fray.

"Mom is a wreck," Sarah overheard her say on the phone. She was in the hallway, trying to sound quiet, but Sarah caught every word. "She's not taking care of the kids. Randy's doing everything. He's just a kid himself. He shouldn't have to be the parent here."

Brandy's voice crackled faintly through the receiver. "What's she doing all day?"

Vanessa's answer was a dagger.

"Drinking. And feeling sorry for herself."

A pause.

"And the kids?"

Vanessa's voice softened. "They're trying. Mark's pretending he's not scared. And Sarah…" Her voice broke, just a little. "Sarah's starting to realize she doesn't have a mom anymore."

Sarah leaned against the wall, the words curling around her like a storm cloud.

She had a mother.

But she was slipping away—faster than anyone could catch her.

And no matter how tightly Sarah clung to the hope that things would get better, a small voice inside whispered the truth:

Maybe they never would.

Chapter 14

Mark sat cross-legged on his bedroom floor, the dim evening light casting long, moody shadows across the carpet. All around him were careful piles—his treasures, his lifelines. Baseball cards yellowed at the corners. A weathered manila envelope stuffed with old stamps. A rusted tin can filled with foreign coins, each one a doorway to somewhere else. Somewhere better.

His fingers moved slowly, reverently. Not sorting so much as remembering. He smoothed out the edge of a dog-eared stamp with the precision of a surgeon, then picked up a dime—his favorite. A 1955 silver Roosevelt, a little scuffed around the rim, the grooves worn smooth in places. Not worth much to anyone else. But to Mark, it was everything.

Dad had given it to him just a few weeks before he died.

He could still hear the sound of his father's hand dipping into his pocket at the end of each day, the familiar jingle of loose change tumbling free.

"See if you can find yourself something rare, kid."

Sometimes it was a wheat penny. Sometimes a Buffalo nickel. Once, it had been a Canadian dollar coin with a loon on the back. Mark had felt like he'd won the lottery.

But there were no more coins now. No more pockets. No more hands to ruffle his hair and call him "champ."

He clenched the dime so tightly it pressed a crescent into his palm.

From the hallway, Sarah's humming floated through the air—soft, off-key, and impossibly sweet. She was always humming these days. Singing to her dolls. Whispering stories under her breath. It was how she coped.

Mark wished he could do that—disappear into make-believe. But something in him had gone quiet since the funeral. Like a door had closed and locked from the inside.

He thought of Saturdays with Dad—those secret, sacred trips to the bait and tackle shop on the edge of town. The front of the store was always the same: rods hanging from the ceiling, dusty Styrofoam coolers, a display of nets tangled beyond repair. But the back? That was something else entirely.

That's where the good stuff lived. Liquor bottles lined up like soldiers. Cigar smoke curling through the air. And on the counter, always, that old cigar box.

Mark had loved that box more than anything.

Dad would hoist him up with one arm, like it was nothing. "Go on," he'd say with a grin. "Pick a winner."

Mark's tiny hands would disappear into the sea of coins—foreign ones with square centers, coins stamped in faded copper, silver ones with faded emperors or ships etched into the surface. He never picked the shiny ones. Those were new. Boring.

He picked the ones that looked like they'd been places.

Now, he searched on his own. In junk drawers. Under couch cushions. In the lining of old jackets. Once, he'd even snuck into John's nightstand, his heart pounding in his throat, hoping to find one last forgotten coin.

He played with the neighborhood kids sometimes. But not often.

They didn't get it. Didn't understand the comfort in holding history in your hand. The weight of something small that used to belong to someone you loved.

They didn't understand how silence could fill a house like smoke. How sometimes, you had to dig for joy. Like it was buried treasure.

A soft knock on the door broke the quiet.

"Mark?"

Sarah.

He shoved the cigar box beneath his bed, wiping his nose on the sleeve of his t-shirt.

"Yeah?"

She peeked in, her stuffed rabbit hanging from one arm, its ears dragging the floor. "You wanna play?"

Mark didn't answer right away. The air felt heavier than it should've. He looked at her—those wide eyes, still full of hope. Still waiting for him to be her protector. Her big brother. Her anchor.

She shifted nervously. "Please?"

He sighed. A long, tired sound that didn't belong in the mouth of a now eight-year-old.

But then he stood.

Sarah's face lit up like a porch light.

She grabbed his hand, tugging him down the hall toward the backyard. "Let's pretend we're treasure hunters!" she giggled.

Mark smiled, just barely, and followed her outside into the fading light.

The sky was melting into pinks and golds. The air still warm, but gentler now. Crickets chirped in the high grass as the sun dipped lower behind the trees. Sarah ran ahead, calling out clues to invisible maps and buried chests. Mark followed, his hand brushing the edge of the dime in his pocket.

He knew the world was different now. Quieter. Meaner. He knew their father wasn't coming back. But maybe—just maybe—for a little while, they could pretend.

Pretend they were still just kids.

Pretend the world was still safe.

Pretend that somewhere, buried deep beneath the silence, there was still something worth finding.

Chapter 15

It was spring—seven months after John Dawson died—and though the chill had lifted from the Kentucky air, the house still felt frozen in place. Outside, the earth was waking up: dogwoods in bloom, the scent of fresh-cut grass floating on the breeze, children's laughter echoing through the neighborhood. But inside the Dawson house, time had gone still. The walls held their breath. The grief hadn't lifted. It had only learned how to settle deeper.

The first time Bill rang the doorbell, Sarah had been painting with the watercolors Nan had gotten her for Christmas. The world was drawn in pastel—stars and hearts and crooked rainbows melting beneath her fingers. She paused, wiping her dusty palms on her shorts, and stood up on tiptoes to peer through the screen door.

A man stood there with a bouquet of roses in his hand.

He stood around six feet tall, rail-thin, with wiry arms that hinted at strength earned from long hours beneath a relentless sun. His skin was deeply tanned—leathery and weathered, etched by years of outdoor labor. Dark hair, slicked carefully back with gel or sweat, revealed a high forehead, sharp cheekbones, and deep-set, calculating eyes that always seemed to be watching. But it was his smile-slow, self-assured, and just a bit too knowing—that unsettled people. Yellowed by years of tobacco stains, it stretched across his face like a promise he had no intention of keeping, a smarmy grin that never quite reached his eyes. When he spoke, his words slid smoothly from his lips, polite enough on the surface but laced with something unsettling-an edge that made others take a careful step backward. He wore a stiff blue plaid shirt tucked too tightly into creased jeans. His cologne-sharp and sour-fought with the sweet perfume of the roses. Sarah tilted her head.

Sarah tilted her head.

"You're Kim's dad," she said flatly.

"Yeah," he replied, like he was waiting for her to invite him in. "Is your mom home, sweetheart?"

She didn't move.

Then Hattie's voice floated down the hallway. "Sarah, who is it?"

She appeared in the doorway a moment later, adjusting her earrings and smoothing the fabric of her floral dress—the one with the tiny violets that John had once called her 'spring dress.' Her lipstick was fresh. Her perfume trailed behind her like a memory.

And without waiting for an answer, Bill stepped inside.

He handed her the roses like they were something sacred. She held them close, closed her eyes, and smiled.

"Oh, Bill... you shouldn't have."

His hand lingered on hers too long. "You look beautiful, Hattie."

Sarah stepped between them.

"Mama, where are you going?"

Hattie leaned down and kissed her daughter's forehead. "Just out for a bit, Tammy is on her way over. I'll be back before dark."

And just like that, they were gone. The screen door creaked shut, and the quiet inside the house shifted into something strange and unwelcome.

The roses didn't disappear. Neither did Bill.

At first, he was just fixing things—tightening the porch rail, clearing the gutters. Then he started staying for dinner. Then he was around nearly every day. Sarah would find his boots by the door, his tools on the counter, his name in her mother's mouth.

One afternoon, his suitcases appeared in the living room. No announcement. Just there, like they'd always been. Old, brown, scuffed along the edges—like him.

Vanessa showed up that evening, her heels echoing across the hardwood like gunshots.

"Seriously, Mom?"

Hattie was sitting on the couch, mending one of Bill's shirts. She didn't even look up.

"You're sewing for him now?"

Hattie's hands kept moving.

Vanessa's voice cracked like a whip. "You moved in the neighbor. The neighbor, Mom. And it hasn't even been a year."

Hattie sighed, finally glancing up. "Vanessa, it's the middle of the day. Lower your voice."

"Lower my voice?" Vanessa laughed bitterly. "Are you kidding me? What the hell is going on with you?"

"You're making a scene," Hattie muttered, tugging at a loose thread.

"I'm making a scene?" Vanessa's voice rose. "You've replaced Dad with the man from across the backyard and act like it's normal. What about Mark? What about Sarah? What are you even doing?"

"I'm trying to survive," Hattie snapped.

Vanessa flinched. Her face twisted—anger, heartbreak, disbelief. She opened her mouth, then shook her head instead and stormed out. The screen door slammed behind her.

Sarah had watched from the hallway. She didn't understand all of it, but she knew this: her mother's eyes didn't shine like they used to. Not since John. Not even with Bill.

That was the last time they saw Vanessa for a long time.

The house changed after that.

Bill started calling it his house. Started walking through the rooms like he'd always been there. He touched things that didn't belong to him—John's tools, John's chair. He even poured whiskey into the glass John had always used for sweet tea.

And Hattie let him.

She laughed louder when he was near. She let him spend the grocery money on beer and bourbon. She let him bring his friends over—men with yellowed teeth and breath that stank of cigarettes and secrets.

They filled the house like smoke, thick and toxic.

They sat in John's living room, where he used to help Mark sort coins and read Sarah bedtime stories. Now, the air was sour with liquor and crude jokes. Sarah learned to stay out of the way.

Then the letter came.

Hattie stood at the sink, her hand trembling as she opened the envelope. She didn't say a word, just stared at the paper for a long time.

The house was in foreclosure.

John had worked his entire life for that house.

And it was slipping away.

Hattie drank more after that. Sometimes she didn't come out of her room for days. Sarah would press her ear to the door and hear nothing but the clink of bottles and the low hum of the TV. Bill never stopped her. He encouraged it. Said it was good for her to "relax."

And Sarah?

She just watched. Quietly. Carefully.

She was five years old. Too young to understand how quickly a home can become something else. How fast someone can replace the ones who came before. How grief, when left unchecked, can rot the foundation of a family.

She watched it all happen. Through cracks in doors. Through silence in rooms. Through the eyes of a forgotten little girl.

And the house—John's house—grew darker by the day.

Chapter 16

Sarah hated shoes.

She understood why grown-ups insisted on them—*You'll step on glass, you'll get worms, you'll catch something*—but none of it mattered. The moment her feet hit the porch, her sneakers were flung off like they'd done something unforgivable. To Sarah, shoes were lies. They muffled the world. They got between her and the realness of things.

There was something sacred about the feeling of dirt on her soles. Damp in the shade, hot in the sun. It grounded her—like she belonged to the land more than the house she lived in. Her toes squished into the mud near the garden hose, brushed over sharp gravel, dug into the clay along the ditch that split the back lots. She felt it all.

It was early morning, and already the Kentucky summer had begun to wrap around the yard like a damp quilt. The air was thick with honeysuckle and buzzing flies, and the sky was that cloudless kind of blue that meant it was going to be another scorcher. But Sarah didn't care.

She had business to attend to.

And no grown-up rules or sulking grief in the house was going to stop her.

"Sarah! Wait up!"

She spun around, her tangled curls flying, and spotted Tommy

Watson puffing down the sidewalk behind her. His knockoff sneakers slapped loudly against the pavement, and his oversized t-shirt clung to him like wet tissue.

Tommy was her best friend. Sometimes. When he wasn't being a pest. He was taller and louder, and sometimes tried to be in charge—but Sarah always found a way to win. She was faster. Smarter. And barefoot.

"You're slow," she shouted, already laughing.

"You got a head start!" he called, trying not to trip over the cracked curb.

Sarah darted ahead, zig-zagging between driveways and front lawns until she reached the edge of what the neighborhood kids called *the woods*—a narrow patch of trees just a few houses down, sandwiched between two empty lots and the remnants of a gravel access road. The subdivision was still half-built, the houses on their block new enough to smell like fresh paint, but this stretch of trees had been here longer—left behind for reasons no one explained. And to Sarah, it may as well have been a forest.

The moment she crossed the threshold between grass and shade, her whole body relaxed. In here, the air felt cooler. Older. Like it had stories to tell.

The clearing at the center held their greatest creation: a half-built fort made of scrap wood, rope, and dreams. Two wooden pallets leaned against each other in a crooked A-frame. Pine branches were wedged across the top like a roof. An old screen door lay flat on the ground like a welcome mat from another life.

Sarah dropped to her knees, wincing only slightly when a sharp stick grazed her shin. Another scab. She was used to it. Her legs looked like a battlefield. Purple bruises, pink scars, raw knees. But Sarah didn't cry over scrapes.

Band-Aids were badges. Scars were trophies.

Tommy plopped beside her, pulling a tangle of twine from his pocket. "Told you I got rope."

She took it, nodding with approval. "We can finish the roof now. And maybe add a window."

He blinked. "How?"

She shrugged. "We'll figure it out."

That's how most things worked in Sarah's world. No plans. Just ideas and grit.

For the next hour, they worked side by side—Tommy holding things steady while Sarah tied knots, climbing onto old milk crates to tuck pine branches into the gaps. They reinforced the walls with broken pieces of lattice from behind her neighbor's shed and used moss to fill in the biggest holes.

They didn't talk much. The birds did it for them.

When Tommy tripped in a tangle of weeds and landed flat on his back, Sarah cackled until her ribs hurt. When she stubbed her toe on a tree root, he handed her a leaf like it might help.

By midmorning, their clothes were soaked with sweat, and their faces were streaked with dirt. Sarah didn't care. She wore the filth like armor.

When it was done—still crooked, still wobbly, but more complete than before—Sarah stepped back and surveyed their masterpiece.

"It's beautiful," she said solemnly, placing a small pinecone on the stump they'd dubbed the table.

Tommy dropped onto the grass and pulled a peanut butter sandwich from his pocket, the wax paper torn and smudged with dirt. "You always gotta be the boss."

Sarah grinned, flopping down beside him. "Somebody's gotta be."

They lay there in the shade, the leaves rustling softly above them.

The sun blinked between branches like a lazy eye, and the cicadas sang their high summer song. Sarah let it all wash over her.

Out here, there were no locked doors. No whispered phone calls. No quiet kitchen chairs or moms who forgot to look you in the eye.

Out here, the world made sense.

Out here, she could be anyone. A builder. A queen. A wild girl who didn't wear shoes and didn't need rules and didn't care if her legs were dirty.

She opened her eyes again, just long enough to look at the sky.

And she wished—quietly, fiercely—that she could stay in the woods forever.

Chapter 17

The heat rose off the pavement in shimmering waves as Sarah sat cross-legged on the porch, a thin sheen of sweat clinging to her freckled skin. The summer of 1979 had already turned Kentucky into a furnace, the air thick and heavy like a wet blanket no one could shake off. The cracked concrete beneath her bare legs burned hot, but she didn't move. Her eyes remained locked on the road ahead, her chin resting on one dirty palm, the other loosely wrapped around her skinny knees.

She was not quite six, and already she had learned what it meant to wait.

This was the third day in a row her mother hadn't come home when she said she would.

Inside the house, Mark sat at the kitchen table with quiet focus, carefully separating his coins into neat piles. He was only seven but had already developed the instincts of someone much older—someone who knew that routine could hold the chaos at bay. The clink of nickels and dimes was a soft, steady rhythm in the otherwise suffocating stillness of the house. A single fly buzzed around the torn screen door. Somewhere down the block, a dog barked once, then fell silent.

Their older brother Randy had left early that morning for work at one of his two jobs. Hattie—*Mommy*—hadn't been seen since she walked out the day before with her purse slung over her shoulder and a cigarette between her fingers.

She had said, *"I'll be back later."*

But later never came.

The neighbor's teenage daughter, Tammy, had been coming by in Hattie's absence. She was seventeen, tall and thin with long legs and hair piled high on her head like the girls on TV. She didn't say much—mostly sat in the armchair with a magazine or flipped channels on the television—but she was there. Watching. Making sure the kids didn't burn the house down or wander too far. She brought over a few slices of white bread and some bologna the day before and told Mark to make sandwiches. Then she'd gone back to painting her nails.

Sarah didn't dislike Tammy. She just didn't trust her quiet.

That morning, Tammy had walked back next door to her own house for "a minute," and hadn't returned. Sarah hadn't gone to look for her. She preferred the porch anyway.

Dinner the night before had been SpaghettiOs—again. Mark had retrieved the can from the low shelf, guiding Sarah's hands to help pour it into the pot. He let her stir carefully over the low flame, watching with the solemn eyes of someone who knew fire could be as dangerous as it was necessary.

It was their third dinner of SpaghettiOs that week. Neither of them mentioned it.

Outside, the sun sagged lower, bleeding orange into the trees and stretching long, skeletal shadows across the yard. Sarah stood and wiped her brow with the back of her arm. Her stomach growled, but she ignored it. Hunger had become a background noise, like the distant rumble of cars on the highway or the whir of the ceiling fan that never quite cooled the room.

A car engine sputtered at the far end of the block, followed by the sharp screech of tires. A man two houses down shouted something angry and indistinct. Then—silence again. A quiet so dense it seemed to buzz in her ears.

Mark appeared in the doorway, silhouetted by the dim interior. "You coming in?" he asked.

She shook her head. "Not yet."

"She's gonna be late again tonight."

Sarah's gaze didn't leave the road. "She might come soon."

Mark didn't argue. He just gave a small nod, his expression unreadable, and stepped back inside.

As the last sliver of sun disappeared behind the trees, Sarah finally stood. Her legs had gone stiff. Dust clung to her calves. She walked inside with slow, reluctant steps, as if crossing some invisible line between hope and disappointment.

The living room was dim, cloaked in the pale amber glow of a single lamp in the corner. The curtains remained drawn, heavy with the scent of old cigarette smoke. Dust floated in the light like ash. The room felt hollow—like it was waiting, too.

Mark was stretched out on the couch, flipping through one of John's old bird field guides. The cover was frayed, the corners soft and bent from years of handling. Their father had loved birds. Sarah didn't know why, but that book always made her feel closer to him, like maybe he'd walk through the door at any moment and quiz her on the difference between a cedar waxwing and a robin.

Tammy had returned at some point and was now half-asleep on the recliner, a half-eaten plate of bologna and crackers on the side table next to a mostly empty can of RC Cola. The TV played some sitcom laugh track no one was watching.

Sarah climbed onto the couch and laid her head on Mark's shoulder. He didn't flinch, just turned a page and kept reading.

"She'll be home soon," Sarah whispered. The words tasted hollow in her mouth, like something she was supposed to say but didn't believe.

Mark shifted slightly. "You want me to make something? There's still peanut butter."

"I'm not hungry," she said, though her stomach ached in protest.

But it wasn't just hunger.

It was *the ache of waiting.* The ache of knowing something was wrong but not being old enough to name it. It sat in her belly like a stone.

Her eyes wandered back toward the window, catching the first flicker of the streetlamp outside. It buzzed softly as it blinked to life, casting long, thin shadows across the worn carpet.

Sarah pressed her small hand against the cool glass of the window-pane. Outside, the world moved on—cars passed, porch lights blinked on, screen doors slammed. But their house remained still. Suspended.

Inside, the silence wrapped around her like a second skin.

And in that silence, the girl in the window watched.

Still waiting.

Chapter 18

The sun beat down on the overgrown yard behind the house, the grass tall enough to tickle bare legs as Sarah and Mark tore through it, laughing as they chased each other with sticks turned into swords. Summer in Kentucky had a way of pressing in—hot and damp and buzzing with cicadas—but out here, it felt like freedom.

There was no garden anymore. No neat rows of tomatoes or cucumbers like there had been when John was alive. The tilled earth had given way to weeds and wild grass, and the shed that once held tools and jars of preserved vegetables now leaned to one side, half-swallowed by vines. Without their father's steady presence, the yard had become just another forgotten thing.

Most mornings, the kids slipped quietly from their beds, careful not to disturb the silence of the house. Hattie rarely stirred before noon these days, and when she did, it was usually for a beer or a cigarette, not breakfast.

Mark would dig through the cabinets and find something—stale cereal, maybe a can of beans—while Sarah sat at the table swinging her legs and brushing tangles from her hair with her fingers. There was no routine anymore, just survival. Once they had eaten, they'd slip out the back door and disappear into the neighborhood.

They played with the kids from down the street—Amy, Josh, Tommy, and sometimes even Roy and Kim. They built forts from scrap wood, raced bikes up and down the street, and dared each other to climb the tallest tree in the vacant lot. No one asked where they came from, and no one asked when they had to leave. It was an unspoken agreement between children: what happened at home stayed there.

By the time the sky turned a dusky purple and the first porch lights flickered on, Mark and Sarah were trudging home, skin sunburned and feet filthy. Sarah had a new scrape on her elbow. Mark's shirt was ripped from climbing a fence. They didn't talk much as they approached the back steps, their laughter quieting with each step toward the house.

Inside, the living room was thick with cigarette smoke and the sour tang of beer. Bill was in John's recliner—John's chair—leaned back like he'd always belonged there. Three other men lounged around the room, their voices booming and their laughter mean. The television blared a ballgame, but no one seemed to be watching.

As the door creaked open, all four men turned.

"There they are," Bill said, his voice slurred but sharp. "Look who finally decided to show up."

Mark stiffened. Sarah instinctively reached for his hand.

"Out runnin' wild all day," Bill continued, his eyes narrowing. "No chores, no nothin'. Just runnin' the streets like a pack of strays."

One of the men chuckled. "Hell, I didn't even know you had kids."

"They aren't my damn kids, they sure as hell don't act like they belong to anyone," Bill muttered, rising to his feet.

He staggered toward them, towering over their small frames. Mark took a step forward, trying to shield Sarah.

"We were just playing," Mark said, voice small but steady.

"Playing?" Bill barked a laugh. "You think the world gives a damn about playin'?"

He didn't wait for an answer. With a sudden swing of his boot, he kicked Mark square in the side, sending him sailing across the room.

Sarah screamed, reaching for him, but Bill grabbed her by the arm and shoved her back.

She tumbled to the carpet, gasping.

The room exploded with laughter. The men clapped their knees, shaking their heads like it was all a great joke.

For a flicker of a second, Sarah looked to her mother. Hattie stood at the edge of the hallway, one hand gripping the doorframe, her face pale and unreadable.

Her eyes met Sarah's.

She said nothing.

"Go on now," Bill barked, waving them off like flies. "Baths. Bed. No supper for little street rats."

Mark pulled himself up, wincing as he took Sarah's hand. Together, they walked down the hall in silence, not daring to look back.

Behind them, the men returned to their drinking. The sound of laughter followed them like a ghost.

That night, Sarah ran the bathwater for herself after Mark had finished. She kept it shallow, dipping in slowly, wincing at the sting where her skin was scraped. The room smelled of old soap and mildew. The faucet dripped a slow, steady beat as she stared at the bubbles gathering around her knees.

In the other room, Mark lay on his bed, a damp towel draped over the footboard. He hadn't said much after they were dismissed, just held his side and blinked at the ceiling.

The house had gone quiet again, save for the murmur of the TV and the clinking of bottles.

They didn't speak. There was nothing to say.

They were no longer just kids.

They were survivors.

Chapter 19

The house had never been quieter.

After the sirens faded and the police cruisers pulled away, the silence crept in like a fog, curling under the door frames and nesting in the corners. Mary and her kids were gone. Penny, Bill's ex-wife still lived in the next court over. She saw what was going on and immediately rushed across the backyard in a panic, dragging Kim and Roy back home by the arms. The chaos had scattered, but the damage lingered—raw and visible.

Hattie sat slumped at the kitchen table, elbows propped against the surface, her face buried in her hands. The beer bottle beside her sweated into a dark ring that matched the stains on the wood. Her robe hung open at the neck, exposing the pale curve of her shoulder. Her eyes were blank.

"Mom?" Sarah whispered from the doorway.

Nothing.

She took a timid step forward, but Mark reached out and grabbed her wrist, holding her back.

"Don't," he muttered, his voice low and tight.

Sarah looked up at him. His face didn't look like Mark's anymore—it looked like someone older. His jaw was locked. His eyes were hard. He wasn't just upset. He was furious.

"She doesn't care," he said. "Not about you. Not about me. Not about any of it."

Sarah didn't say anything. She just stared at the slumped figure of her mother, waiting for her to move. To speak. To be someone again.

But she didn't.

Randy came home late. The porch light flickered overhead, casting tired shadows across his face. Billy, Gertie's son, had met him in the driveway, wide-eyed with the story of what had happened. Eight cruisers. Guns drawn. Bill and Keith cuffed in the grass.

Randy didn't even put down his bag. He walked straight into the kitchen and stopped cold.

Hattie didn't look up.

"So it's true," he said, voice like flint striking steel.

She blinked, slow and unseeing.

"Bill's in jail. Keith, too. You gonna tell me what they were doing? Where that money came from? Or do I need to guess?"

She flinched, just barely.

"God, Mom," he snapped, stepping forward. "What the hell is wrong with you?"

Her fingers curled tighter around the bottle.

Randy slammed his hand down on the table. "They could've shot Mark. Or Sarah. You let that into our house!"

"Don't talk to me like that," she slurred, but the fight in her voice had already vanished.

"No one else will," he said. "So I will. Look at this place. Look at yourself."

He gestured around the kitchen—the empty bottles, the cigarette burns on the floor, the pizza boxes stacked like tombstones.

"At this rate, you'll be dead before summer."

That did it.

Her shoulders crumpled. Her head bowed. But Randy was already turning, already halfway down the hallway, his door slamming like a final word.

Sarah stood frozen in the shadows. Her chest felt tight.

Hattie didn't even look at her.

The house felt smaller after that. Like it was closing in. The walls seemed to lean, like they were tired of holding up so much grief. More pink notices appeared on the door, fluttering like dying birds in the breeze. Disconnect notices. Eviction warnings.

But Hattie didn't notice.

She wasn't home most days. When she was, she brought the bar with her—liquor on her breath, slurred apologies that meant nothing, loud fights with no one in particular. She'd collapse on the couch by sundown, one leg draped over the armrest like a broken doll.

Randy started staying out later. Working more shifts. Sleeping less. Every time he passed Hattie on the way to the bathroom or the kitchen, he looked like he wanted to scream—but didn't. Like yelling at her one more time would only make him disappear, too.

Mark and Sarah learned how to vanish.

Each morning, they slipped outside as early as they could, pockets full of crackers or dry cereal they'd scavenged from the nearly empty pantry. They stayed gone as long as the sun let them, clinging to neighborhood friendships that dulled the ache.

They rode bikes around the block until their legs burned. Played hide-and-seek until the streetlights blinked on. Josh and Amy some friends that lived down the street, had a tire swing behind their house, and sometimes they all lay on it together, staring up at the sky, making up constellations and pretending they were far, far away.

When they came home, they never knew what they'd walk into. Some nights Hattie wasn't there at all. Other nights she'd be passed out on the couch with the TV blaring. Either way, they'd tiptoe down the hall, brush their teeth in silence, and crawl into bed without turning on the lights.

But one night, Randy picked up the phone.

He didn't pace. He didn't rant.

He just stood in the kitchen, one hand on the counter, the other holding the receiver.

When Their grandmother, Nan, answered, her voice cracked softly across the line: "Hello?"

He didn't know what to say at first. But he didn't need to.

She already knew.

"Nan," he whispered, his voice thick. "We need you."

Help was coming.

But they had no idea how much they'd need her.

Or how little time they had left.

Chapter 20

February 1980. The frost had begun to lift, but winter still lingered in the shadows of early morning. Sidewalks wore a thin dusting of salt, and the breath of schoolchildren puffed like tiny ghosts into the crisp air. It had been seven months since the police came for Bill—seven months of fragile, hollow quiet. Sarah had just started second grade, and Mark was in fifth. The seasons had changed, but inside the Dawson house, grief still clung to the walls like soot.

Nan was there most days now.

Her presence brought something steady. Not peace, not exactly—but structure. A soft barrier between chaos and collapse. When Nan stayed, the house didn't feel like it was teetering. She brought routines with her—real meals, folded laundry, kids getting to school on time. She slept in Sarah's bed, her curved spine curled like a question mark, her breath raspy and uneven. She grunted when she moved, but her presence filled the house in a way Hattie no longer could.

The cancer had spread, Sarah had overheard. No one said it directly, but she could tell. The way Nan winced when she shifted her weight. The way Hattie's hands trembled while changing the dressing on the angry lesion that lived on Nan's back like a secret. Sarah helped with the gauze. She never flinched. Her small hands stayed steady, her eyes focused. She did as she was told.

"You've got gentle hands," Nan would whisper. "You're taking good care of me."

Sometimes, in the haze of afternoon, Hattie and Nan would sit side by side in front of the television. They drank tall beers and smoked Winstons while soap opera voices drifted like lullabies through the kitchen. It felt almost normal. Like maybe, somehow, they were rebuilding something.

Until the morning Nan didn't get out of bed.

Sarah noticed first.

The bedroom was still and dark. No rustling of bedsheets. No call for help with the bandage. No smell of coffee or the clink of a cigarette lighter.

"She's probably just tired," Hattie muttered when Sarah said something. "Leave her be."

But as the sun rose higher, even Hattie's voice lost its certainty.

That night, Sarah was told she'd be sleeping with her mother.

"No argument," Hattie said, already laying out her pajamas on the couch. Her tone was firm. Her face was pale. She didn't meet Sarah's eyes.

"Is Nan okay?" Sarah asked, her voice small.

"She's just not feelin' good." Hattie's words snapped shut like a drawer.

That night, Sarah curled into her mother's bed, her body stiff and unsure. The sheets smelled like Aqua Net and old cigarettes. Hattie's breathing was uneven. Sarah stayed awake long after the house went quiet, blinking into the dark.

At some point, she thought she heard voices—low and unfamiliar. The floor creaked. A zipper clicked. The refrigerator door opened and closed. But when she woke in the morning, the house was silent.

Hattie was already dressed. Her eyes were ringed in red. She said nothing except, "Get ready. You're going to school."

"But what about Nan?" Sarah asked, rubbing the sleep from her eyes.

"She's not here anymore," Hattie replied, her voice flat. "She had to go."

Sarah blinked. "Go where?"

But Hattie didn't answer. She just shoved a sandwich into Sarah's backpack and called for Mark to hurry.

There was no crying. No goodbyes. Just silence and motion. As if pretending fast enough would make the truth stay behind.

It wasn't until they came home from school that Hattie told them. She sat them down at the kitchen table, her hands wrapped around a mug that no longer steamed.

"She passed in her sleep," she said. "Peacefully."

Sarah stared at the table. Mark didn't move.

The funeral was scheduled for Friday.

That Friday was also the school Valentine's Day party.

Sarah's class was decorating cupcakes and cutting hearts out of pink construction paper. Her desk was covered in glitter and confetti and little plastic baggies of candy.

But all she could think about was Nan.

She wondered if they'd let her wear the faded housecoat she always loved—the pink one with the missing buttons. She wondered if her eyes had stayed open. If anyone had brushed her hair.

She wondered why she wasn't there.

"You're going to school," Hattie had said. "It's not a place for little girls."

And so, Sarah went.

She sat in class with a red paper crown on her head and a desk full of uneaten candy. Outside, rain tapped against the windows, soft and steady. Her teacher read a poem about love. The other kids giggled and passed notes. But Sarah didn't move.

Her eyes stayed fixed on the gray blur outside. On the way the world kept turning.

Nan was gone. And no one noticed but her.

She had a mother. But she was alone.

Chapter 21

The air inside the house had turned rancid—thick with stale beer, old sweat, and cigarette smoke that never fully cleared. The kitchen, once a space where Hattie Dawson had stirred oatmeal and tucked lunchbox napkins with quiet love, now reeked of rot. Greasy pizza boxes sagged on the counter. Beer bottles—some half-full—lined the windowsill like trophies. Ashtrays overflowed onto yellowing placemats, and the light above the sink flickered like it, too, wanted out.

Hattie sat slouched at the kitchen table, one arm draped across it, the other clutching a warm bottle by the neck. Her hair hung limp, a curtain shielding bloodshot eyes that barely tracked the room around her. And yet, she was laughing—high-pitched and brittle—like something sharp splitting under pressure. Bill leaned in beside her, whispering into her ear, his voice low and greasy. Every few seconds, she'd cackle again, the sound echoing too loud in the small kitchen.

Across from them, Bill's brother Keith leaned back in a chair, boots propped on the table like he owned the place. His girlfriend Mary twirled her hair and laughed at nothing, her lipstick smudged and her eyes glossy. They didn't look like guests. They looked like squatters who'd carved out a kingdom from someone else's ruin.

"I'm going to lose the house, Bill," Hattie slurred, her fingers twitching around the bottle's neck.

"If I lose this house…"

Bill waved her off. "You worry too much."

There was no reassurance in his voice. Just dismissal.

"What can we do to help?" Mary cooed, not bothering to look up from her drink.

No one meant any of it.

The truth was simple: they were drowning. And no one was swimming toward the surface.

The pink eviction notices had stopped being warnings. Now, they were certainties. Piled up on the table. Jammed into drawers. Wedged behind nearly empty boxes of cereal and packs of Menthols. Time was running out, and everyone knew it—but nobody moved.

"Let's roll," Keith suddenly barked, slapping Bill on the back. He was already up, moving fast.

"Where are you going?" Hattie called after him, her voice unraveling.

"We'll be back," Bill muttered, grabbing his jacket.

The front door slammed. And just like that, they were gone.

Hattie didn't ask where. She didn't want to know.

Down the hall, the children had retreated into Mark's room. It had once belonged only to him and Sarah—safe, quiet, theirs. But now it was overrun.

"Get out of my stuff, Kim!" Mark snapped, lunging as Kim yanked one of his action figures off the dresser.

"I'm just looking," she whined.

"Yeah, well look somewhere else."

Roy, sprawled across the bed, peeled through Mark's baseball cards with greasy fingers, bending corners like they were junk mail. Sarah sat on the floor beside the dresser, clutching her stuffed rabbit and staring at the peeling wallpaper. Her dolls were missing. Her books were scattered. Even the blanket Nan had crocheted now lay balled in the closet corner.

Kim and Roy weren't just visiting anymore. They were claiming the space. Claiming everything.

Then came the sound of boots stomping on linoleum.

Mark and Sarah froze.

Bill and Keith had returned. And this time, they brought something with them.

In the kitchen, the thud of a heavy bag hitting the table made the whole floor vibrate.

"What the hell..." Mary breathed.

The kids crept into the hallway, peeking from behind the cracked door.

Crumpled up cash and change spilled from the duffel bag. Crumpled bills. Rolled twenties. Hundreds tucked in rubber bands.

Mary ran her hands through it like it was water. "Damn," she whispered. "Where'd you two hit the jackpot?"

Bill didn't answer. Neither did Keith. Hattie didn't ask. She just stared at the money like it was a loaded gun. Her hand trembled as she grabbed an empty coffee can and shoved the cash inside. She quickly stuffed the can in the freezer.

Sarah and Mark exchanged a look.

Something was wrong.

The heat crept through the open windows, thick as breath. The television buzzed low in the bedroom, the screen flickering in the dark. Having returned to the bedroom, Mark sat cross-legged on the floor with Sarah beside him. They shared a bag of stale chips they'd scavenged from the kitchen cabinet.

And then—sirens.

Bright, flashing lights cut across the wallpaper. Red. Blue. Red again.

"What's that?" Kim asked, already scrambling to the window.

"Cops," Mark whispered.

Sarah's stomach twisted. She remembered the sound of police radios from long ago. From when John got sick. From when everything started unraveling.

Mark turned off the TV. "Get away from the window," he ordered.

They crouched in the shadows as doors slammed and shouts echoed from the porch.

"Hands where I can see 'em!"

Boots thundered across the front steps. A woman screamed. Glass shattered.

Sarah peered through the blinds, just once.

Hattie was barefoot in her nightgown, mascara streaked like war paint down her cheeks. She was clinging to Bill's arm like he was her last lifeline. Begging. Crying. Screaming his name as officers cuffed him and Keith.

But the police didn't flinch.

"Turn around!" they barked. "Hands behind your back!"

Mark tugged Sarah away from the window.

Suddenly, another voice rose sharply above the noise. "Where is it, Hattie? We know you're hiding the money."

Sarah froze. She looked back toward the window, heart hammering.

"I don't know what you're talking about," her mother shrieked, shaking her head violently. Her wild hair whipped around her face, tears spilling from wide, terrified eyes.

A flashlight beam sliced through the doorway, illuminating the porch and painting harsh shadows on the walls.

"Mrs. Dalton," a different officer said, stepping closer, his voice calmer but edged with warning. "If you don't give us that money back, you're gonna be going downtown with them."

"I don't have anything!" Hattie cried, her voice cracking. "Leave me alone!"

"We know it's here," the officer pressed again, his tone cold, relentless. "This is your last chance. If we find it without your help, you're going to jail right alongside Bill."

Hattie stood rigid, shoulders trembling. Silence stretched between them, thick as the summer heat. Then, slowly, she lifted her chin, eyes hardened with defiance and desperation.

"I told you-I don't have it."

Sarah pulled away from Mark, creeping back to the window just as an officer moved toward the doorway. He loomed over Hattie, flashlight slicing across her frightened face.

"Mrs. Dalton," he said again, voice firm but quiet, "we're not playing games here. Give us the money now, or you'll be in cuffs."

Hattie stared at him, chest rising and falling rapidly, breath hitching with fear. Her eyes flickered toward Bill, already restrained, his head bowed in defeat. Slowly, she pressed one trembling hand against her mouth, mascara smudged into dark streaks down her cheeks.

The officer exhaled sharply and nodded to another policeman standing nearby. "Search the whole place. Tear it apart."

"Alright," she finally whispered, voice barely audible. "I'll give it to you."

The officer held up a hand to stop the officers before they entered the house.

Sarah watched, her breath tight in her throat, as her mother disappeared into the shadows of the house. Moments later, Hattie returned clutching a crumpled envelope tightly against her chest, like a secret she couldn't bear to reveal. She hesitated, her knuckles white with tension, before slowly extending her arm toward the officer.

"Here," she said softly, her voice breaking. "Take it."

The policeman took the envelope from her gently, opening it to glance quickly inside before nodding to the others. As he turned away, Hattie folded inward, wrapping her arms tightly around herself as though she'd given away the last piece of something she desperately needed.

Sarah stood motionless at the window, her heart aching as she watched her mother crumble silently onto the porch steps, shoulders shaking. The house was still again, but it wasn't theirs anymore. It belonged to the flashing lights, the heavy boots, and the shadowed memories that Sarah knew would never leave.

Sarah felt Mark's hand grip her shoulder, gently pulling her back again. They sank into the shadows, pressed tight together as Kim whimpered softly in the corner and Roy stared blankly at the wall. The house-their house-was no longer a home.

Sarah clutched her knees to her chest, eyes burning.

She had never seen her mother cry like that for John.

She had never cried that way for them.

Only for Bill.

For the man who had hit them, mocked them, taken their food, and wrecked what little was left of their lives.

And Sarah, barely five and a half years old, felt something unfamiliar rise up in her chest-hot and fierce and aching.

Shame.

Not for herself.

For her mother.

She buried her face in her brother's shirt.

And the only thought in her head was this:

Daddy would never have let this happen.

Chapter 22

It had been nearly ten months since the night flashing lights took Bill and Keith away, and the silence that followed should've felt like peace. But peace, they'd learned, was never built to last.

Bill had taken a plea deal—five years in prison. No trial. No drawn-out drama. Just one courtroom appearance, a set of handcuffs, and the bang of a gavel. When the verdict came down, Hattie collapsed in the kitchen, wailing into a dishtowel like someone had ripped her heart out. But the kids didn't cry. They just looked at each other in quiet disbelief, and relief. For them, it was spring again—not outside, but inside. A reprieve from the chaos. The shouting, the fists, the men with cigarette burns and cruel eyes—they were gone.

And for a little while, life settled.

But grief has a way of finding new cracks to slip into.

Two months later, Nan had died.

She had been the thread barely holding them together. When she was gone, the seams burst wide open. Hattie unraveled fast—drinking harder, sleeping longer, disappearing for days. There was no one left to soften the blow.

Then came the foreclosure notice.

The house was officially gone.

John's house. Nan's house. The place that had once smelled like fresh-cut grass and cinnamon toast. It all slipped through Hattie's fingers like dust. And all she did was curse the mailbox and pop another tab off a beer.

She found them a three-bedroom apartment tucked between chain-link fences and broken promises, just inside the city limits. The carpet smelled like mildew. The bathroom light flickered. But it had a roof. That was enough—for now.

Hattie claimed the master bedroom. Randy took the second. Mark and Sarah were left with the smallest one—just big enough for two beds and a cracked window that let in more noise than air. They didn't complain. By then, they knew better.

Their new school was miles away. But Hattie didn't transfer their records—didn't want the hassle. So each morning, Sarah and Mark pulled on their shoes and started walking. A mile and a half through cracked sidewalks and damp Kentucky mornings. It didn't matter if it rained or snowed. They walked.

It wasn't fair. But fair had nothing to do with survival.

That summer came in thick—air heavy with heat and the buzz of cicadas. The pavement sizzled. Apartment doors stayed open to catch the faintest breeze. Hattie found new drinking buddies, and by mid-June, she was drinking more than she was speaking.

She brought strangers home. Laughed too loud. Forgot to cook.

Mark stayed out late with boys who hung around the parking lot, skating over potholes and daring each other to jump the broken fence. Sarah wandered. No girls her age, no one to follow, so she invented games in the gravel lot and listened quietly to the grownups on the balcony as they bragged and slurred and didn't notice her.

Randy worked. He showered. He slept. That was it. He hardly spoke, but his presence was still an anchor in the storm.

Then one night, fire tore through the building behind theirs.

Randy had just come home, sweat still clinging to his collar, when he saw the smoke. Without hesitation, he ran straight into it—kicked in the door of an elderly woman's apartment and dragged her out just before the flames took hold.

Neighbors screamed. Sirens split the air.

By morning, his face was in the paper. The news came with a headline: *"Local Man Saves Elderly Woman From Apartment Fire."* People clapped when he walked by. Kids asked for autographs. Randy just shrugged it off, went to work the next day like nothing had changed.

But Sarah noticed. Something had changed. For once, people were seeing the version of him she'd always known.

And then it all came crashing down—again.

It happened on a day too hot for anything but trouble. Hattie and a few of her new friends were packed onto the apartment balcony, laughing, drinking, half-hanging off rusted railings. Sarah came out barefoot, a simple question on her lips.

She didn't see the beer can.

Her foot nudged it. The can tumbled, hit the decking below and spilled onto the man in the unit underneath.

His shout shot up like a gunshot.

Within minutes, he was pounding on the door, red-faced and spitting threats. Hattie laughed at first. Thought it was funny. But the man didn't. He called the manager. And the manager had already been waiting for a reason.

Late rent. Noise complaints. Too many warnings.

The eviction notice came the next morning, flapping in the breeze like a white flag of surrender.

No pleading. No extensions. Just a date and a deadline.

And once again, they were nowhere. Drifting.

Sarah stood on the balcony that night, watching the sun go down behind the smoke-stained roofs of a place that never felt like home. Her bare feet were black with dirt. Her arms were crossed tight over her chest.

Another address gone. Another chapter closed.

Only this time, she wasn't afraid.

She was tired.

And ready.

Because now, she understood something no child ever should:

Home wasn't a place. It was the space between what was lost and what hadn't yet been taken.

And there was less and less of it every day.

Chapter 23

Randy didn't move with them.

It wasn't exactly his choice—but it wasn't really his decision either.

One quiet morning, while he was at work grinding through a double shift, Hattie packed up the apartment with the help of two of her drinking buddies. She rented a dented U-Haul from across town, loaded what little they owned with Mark and Sarah trailing silently behind, and left.

No warning. No goodbye.

When Randy came home that night, the apartment was hollow. Just a few empty beer cans scattered across the stained carpet, a forgotten ashtray on the kitchen counter, and the lingering sour smell of smoke and spilled beer. Everything else—gone.

Except his own things, which she'd left behind like they were an afterthought. His clothes stacked in the corner of his bedroom. His tools lined up on the dresser. The bed still made.

Taped to the door was a single sheet of paper, curling at the edges from the humidity. Hattie's scrawled handwriting cut through the quiet like a slap:

Couldn't afford the rent anymore. Had to downsize. New address: Lisa Gardens Apartments, Building 4, Unit 108. —Mom.

That was it.

No apology. No explanation. No mention of how she could walk out on him the way she had.

Randy stood there in the doorway, the note fluttering faintly in the breeze from the busted window unit, his jaw clenched so tight his teeth ached. He didn't cry. Didn't scream. Just stood in the silence that wrapped around him like a noose.

He stared into the vacant space, where echoes of his siblings still clung to the air—the thud of Mark's footsteps, Sarah's soft humming—and felt the floor give way beneath him.

But he didn't follow.

Couldn't.

His heart ached for Mark and Sarah. But he knew he couldn't be what they needed. Not yet. Not like they deserved. So he let the guilt settle into his chest, a leaden weight he carried quietly.

The new apartment was a downgrade in every way.

A bottom-floor basement unit at the back of a sagging complex, wedged between the roar of the highway and behind a grocery store. The view was nothing but dumpsters and broken glass. The windows sat high on the walls—barely big enough to let in a slice of gray daylight—and the walls forever smelled like mildew and someone else's fried food.

Inside, it was dim and claustrophobic. Every room felt smaller than the last.

But Hattie didn't care.

The second the U-Haul was emptied, she cracked open a beer, kicked off her shoes, and claimed the living room as her personal dive bar. Within a week, the apartment was overrun with her new drinking crowd. The air thickened with cigarette smoke and sour breath. Laughter rang through the walls, sharp and hollow, bouncing off the cracked plaster like the echo of a life that was never coming back.

The fridge was always stocked—with beer.

But the cupboards were bare.

Mark and Sarah were left to fend for themselves.

Some days, Hattie dragged them along—tossing them into the back seat of whatever car she'd climbed into for the day, driving to dingy bars with the vinyl seats burning their legs, sweat sticking to the backs of their thighs as they sat in silence, waiting for her to stumble out hours later.

But most days, she left them behind.

There weren't many kids at the new complex.

Mark drifted toward the rougher boys who hung around the parking lot, racing bikes between rusted-out cars and daring each other to scale the chain-link fence behind the dumpsters. Sarah tagged along when she could. But she was smaller—too small to keep up. No girls her age. No one to follow.

So she made her own rules.

She walked the same looping path over the cracked pavement, barefoot and quiet, tracing circles like she was trying to wear a trail into the world that wouldn't disappear. She dug holes in the patchy grass near the dumpsters, searching for lost treasures. And when the boredom settled too deep, she'd dig through the couch cushions, fingers blackened with lint and grime, searching for coins dropped by careless strangers.

At first, it was a game.

Then it became survival.

Every handful of coins meant one more trip to the store, half a mile down the broken sidewalk. Mark always picked the same thing: Ramen noodles—cheap and filling. Sarah craved the crunch of iceberg lettuce or a cucumber—something fresh, something that tasted like more than survival.

They paid in coins. Stacks of copper and nickels counted slowly at the checkout, their fingers sticky with sweat and heat.

The clerks never asked.

They learned to survive on less.

At night, the walls seemed to close in.

The apartment filled with noise—the clink of bottles, the scrape of chairs, the low rumble of men's voices, sharp and slurred. Laughter too loud, too long, never reaching the eyes. There was no space to hide. No doors thick enough to block out the way the voices turned, thick with something that made Sarah's skin crawl.

And when it got too close, too loud, she stood her ground.

Seven years old. Barefoot in the middle of the living room. A slip of a girl with tangled hair and fire in her eyes.

"Get out."

Her voice cut through the smoke, sharp and clear.

Sometimes they laughed.

"Feisty," they'd sneer. "Just like her mama."

But she didn't flinch.

She didn't back down.

And eventually, they left. Muttering. Slamming doors behind them.

Hattie never stopped them. Never even looked up.

"You're such a little troublemaker, Sarah," she'd slur from her chair, eyes glassy, bottle tipping in her lap.

Sarah didn't care.

She wasn't doing it for thanks.

She did it because someone had to.

Someone had to hold the line.

And if no one else would—then it would be her.

II

Part Two

Nobody Came for Us
It wasn't just a new chapter. It was a whole new nightmare.

Chapter 24

Steve was sixteen years younger than Hattie.

At 6'2" and 275 pounds, he towered over her, his broad frame filling doorways like a warning. Once, he'd been a Marine—but the discipline never stuck. Authority was something Steve couldn't stomach. He went AWOL, couldn't stay put, couldn't take orders. Dishonorably discharged. Kicked out like the stray he'd always been.

He had a daughter, Sheila, from a failed marriage-a girl born with cerebral palsy. He never visited. Never paid a cent. Sheila's mother never asked.

And there was a son, too.

Evan.

A near-clone of Steve—same hard jaw, same cold eyes. A boy still young enough to idolize the man who called himself his father.

But the first time Sarah met Steve, she didn't know all that. She only knew what her gut told her.

Something was wrong.

He hadn't said anything cruel. He smiled, even—tight, rehearsed, like someone who'd practiced what a smile was supposed to look like. But his eyes stayed flat. Lifeless. He shook hands too firmly. His laugh exploded into the room, brash and jarring, like a jackhammer breaking the silence.

It was the kind of wrong you couldn't explain—only feel.

He slid into their lives like a shadow, moving slow and silent until one day he was everywhere. Sitting at their kitchen table. Rearranging the furniture. Doing whatever he wanted.

Hattie met him at a bar.

Sarah overheard her slurring to Mary one night, "He's different. He takes care of me."

But even at seven years old, Sarah knew better.

Men who "took care" of you never smiled at your children like that.

At first, Steve wore a mask.

He cleaned. Fixed the loose cabinet door. Helped Hattie with the stack of unpaid bills that had gathered dust. He even made her laugh— a brittle, foreign sound that hadn't lived in their house since John.

But masks only last so long.

"This place is filthy," he muttered one afternoon, glancing around the apartment like the walls offended him.

Hattie stood nearby, arms folded across her chest, nodding like she agreed.

"There's no time like the present," Steve added, voice smooth as glass but sharp underneath. His eyes cut to Sarah and Mark. "You kids better get to work."

They swept. Scrubbed. Scoured the cracked linoleum until their hands burned. But Steve's eyes found fault in everything—a missed crumb under the table, a smudge on the window.

"Do it again," he'd snap.

And they did.

Not because they wanted to. But because they'd already seen what happened when they didn't.

Hattie never stopped him. Never even looked their way. She stood by the counter with a beer clutched in one hand, her gaze distant, like she wasn't there at all.

It happened in a breath.

Sarah and Mark were in Hattie's bedroom, sorting through her closet-bagging up old dresses, folding worn-out shirts. Hattie sat on the side of the bed, the smell of beer thick on her breath.

"I'm tired, Steve," she mumbled. "Why don't you do it yourself?"

Silence.

Too sharp. Too sudden.

Steve's jaw clenched. His shoulders tensed like a loaded spring.

"What did you just say?" His voice was calm. Deadly calm.

"I said—"

The crack of his hand across her face snapped the air in two.

Hattie's head snapped sideways, her hand flying to her cheek as she fell backwards on the bed. She didn't scream. Didn't cry. She sat there, blinking like she'd been slapped by a ghost.

Steve turned to the kids, voice flat. "Get back to work."

And that was it.

Sarah's small hands trembled as she gathered the bags. Mark's jaw tightened, his eyes burning—but he didn't speak.

They finished their work and fled the room, their hearts pounding.

Nothing was the same after that.

"We're movin'," Steve announced one afternoon, like it was just another chore on a list.

No one argued.

Hattie zipped her suitcase shut without looking at her children. Mark and Sarah packed their clothes in garbage bags, their small hands folding shirts like soldiers preparing for war.

The shack squatted at the end of a gravel road—five battered houses lined up like forgotten relics, boxed in by warehouses and factory lots. Vines choked the walls. The porch sagged like a broken promise.

Inside, the floors groaned underfoot. The windows were cracked, streaked with grime. A wood stove, rusted and cold, hunched in the middle of the living room like it had given up long ago.

"This is home now," Steve muttered, tossing a box onto the floor.

Sarah swallowed her tears, gripping Mark's hand tighter than she ever had.

Hell had a new address.

And monsters didn't need to hide anymore.

The shack became a cage.

Steve locked the doors, bolted the windows. "Too dangerous outside," he said, his voice dripping with false concern.

But inside was worse.

Inside was where the monster lived.

Hattie drank. All day. Every day. She hovered near Steve like a moth to a flame, her light dimming with every hour. She cleaned. She cooked. She kept her head down.

Steve drank too. A weird combination of beer and tomato juice, or very old Barton and coke over ice. With a beer in his hand, he laughed too loud and stumbled through stories-but when the whiskey came out, so did the monster, sharp-eyed and mean, lurking just beneath the burn.

The air inside the shack grew heavy, thick with fear. A silence so loud it made Sarah's stomach hurt.

She and Mark learned to read Steve's moods like weather patterns. The slam of the fridge door. The pace of his boots on the floor. The hiss of the stove burner.

And when the storm came, they scattered.

No one came looking for them.

Not the neighbors.

Not the family.

Not even Hattie.

The world beyond the shack faded. And all that remained was survival.

Chapter 25

That night, the shack felt colder, like the walls were holding their breath, waiting for something to happen.

Even though the sticky heat of summer clung to the air outside, inside it hung heavy with something else-tension so thick it stole the breath from the room.

Mark and Sarah sat pressed together on the sagging couch, their eyes fixed on the flickering television, its light casting distorted shadows along the warped paneling. But neither of them was watching. The images flashed and blurred, meaningless.

They could feel it in their bones.

Something was coming.

Steve had been gone all day. That wasn't unusual-he disappeared for hours at a time, running his "business," he had begun using the Social Security check meant to take care of Mark and Sarah and invested it into drug trafficking. But Hattie-Hattie was the reason the air felt poisoned tonight.

She sat at the table near the door, cradling her koozie covered beer, her foot tapping uncontrollably against the floor. Her eyes darted to the clock every few minutes, watching the hours creep by, each tick louder than the last.

Waiting.

Mark noticed it too. He leaned closer to Sarah, his voice barely a whisper.

"Why's she acting so weird?"

Sarah shook her head, her mouth dry. "I don't know," she whispered back, but the knot in her stomach said everything.

Whatever it was-it wasn't good.

The knock came soft. Hesitant.

Hattie bolted upright. Her chair scraped across the floor with a sharp screech. She turned to the kids, her voice tense.

"Stay here."

She opened the door just a crack, shielding whoever stood outside from their view.

But the voice floated in-soft, familiar.

"Hey, Hattie."

Bill.

Sarah's stomach dropped. Her skin prickled as the air tightened.

No. Please. No.

"I just needed to talk," Bill said, his voice carrying that same smooth charm that had always made Sarah uneasy. "I miss you."

For a moment, Hattie hesitated, her shoulders stiff. But then something crumbled in her eyes-something Sarah hadn't seen in months.

Longing.

And then she stepped aside.

"Come in."

Mark's hand shot out, squeezing Sarah's until her knuckles turned white. His voice trembled.

"This is bad."

Sarah nodded, too afraid to speak.

Less than an hour later, the door slammed open.

Steve.

The second he crossed the threshold, the air snapped taut. His eyes locked on Bill like a predator catching scent of blood.

"What the fuck is he doing here?"

Bill stood slowly, his hands raised halfway in mock peace. "Just here to talk."

Steve's laugh came sharp, dangerous. "You think you can just show up here?"

And then the room erupted.

Steve lunged, slamming Bill hard into the wall, the thin paneling shuddering beneath the impact. Bottles crashed to the floor. Hattie screamed. The two men grappled, fists flying, bodies crashing into the coffee table, sending shards of glass skittering across the floor.

Mark dragged Sarah behind the couch, their hearts thudding so loud they drowned out the chaos.

"Stop it!" Hattie cried, rushing toward them.

"You're next, Bitch!" Steve bellowed, shoving her aside like a ragdoll.

The fight spilled across the room-Bill swinging wild, Steve overpowering him. Blood smeared the walls, staining the wooden paneling.

And then-Steve vanished into the back room.

Mark's breath caught. "No…"

When Steve reappeared, his fist gripped something small. Silver. Cold.

A pistol.

"You wanna play games, Bill?" Steve's voice was low, lethal.

Bill's face drained of color, his hands trembling.

"Put it down, Steve."

"You had your chance."

Bill bolted.

BANG!

Somehow, Bill made it.

Tires screeched. He was gone.

Steve stood in the yard, wild-eyed, chest heaving, gun still in hand. "Fuck!"

Mark didn't wait. He grabbed Sarah's hand and pulled her down the hall. They didn't argue. They didn't look back.

They ran.

—-

A few seconds later, Hattie stood in the doorway, staring at Steve.

Slowly, she began to back away.

Seeing that, Steve charged.

She locked the door just in time.

"Open this door!" he bellowed. "Fucking bitch, open the goddamn door!"

He rammed his shoulder against it until the door splintered inward. He grabbed Hattie by the hair and began to beat her-on the head, the back-anywhere he could land a blow.

Sarah had barely crawled into bed when she heard the heavy tread of Steve's boots stomping toward the kitchen. Hattie's voice followed, low and trembling.

Then her screams echoed through the tiny shack.

Mark and Sarah huddled in their beds, pretending to sleep.

They couldn't let Steve see them awake.

The violence spilled into the bedroom. Hours passed. Sarah and Mark could only listen.

Sarah held her breath.

"You fucking whore!" Steve snarled.

Hattie's voice cracked. "I didn't know he was coming, Steve. Please…"

CRASH.

A table overturned. A glass shattered.

Then the pounding of fists.

Sarah curled tighter beneath the thin blanket, squeezing her eyes shut as her mother's screams echoed down the hall.

Through the thin walls, they heard the argument spiral into something darker.

Steve's voice.

"Prove you love me."

"What do you want me to do?" Hattie sobbed.

"You're gonna suck my dick."

"What? No! I wouldn't even do that for John!"

"You will for me or I'll blow your fucking brains out!"

Sarah held her breath, frozen. Powerless.

The sound that followed would haunt her forever.

Sarah pressed her hands over her ears, but the sounds bled through. Hattie's broken cries. Steve's snarling rage. The creak of the bed. The slap of skin, the gagging.

Mark's body was rigid in the top bunk, fists clenched so tight they shook.

When the sounds finally quieted, Sarah barely dared to breathe.

But Steve wasn't finished.

Steve berated her, accused her of thinking she was too good for him.

Then he dragged her by the hair back into the kitchen.

"Get up," he barked. "Clean this shit up."

Hattie sobbed. "I love you, Steve."

"Yeah, you do."

The scrape of a chair. The shuffle of feet. Then the thud of Steve's body collapsing into a chair, the sound of his breath eventually slowing, soft snoring replacing the violence.

But the air stayed thick. Heavy.

Sarah listened as Hattie crumpled onto the kitchen floor, her cries soft and broken.

Somewhere in the dark, Mark whispered:

"We'll survive this."

Sarah nodded, eyes wide open.

Because there was no other choice.

They had to.

Chapter 26

Everything felt different the next night.

Quieter.

But not the good kind of quiet.

It was the kind of silence that came after a storm-the eerie, suffocating stillness that made your skin crawl because you knew it wasn't really over. It was the kind of quiet that listened, waiting to erupt again.

Mark and Sarah lay in their bunk beds-Mark on the top, Sarah tucked below-both wide awake in the heavy stillness. The old frame creaked when either of them moved, so they stayed as still as possible, listening.

The hallway light cast long shadows that stretched across the cracked paneling, flickering as moths bumped against the bare bulb outside the door.

Sarah stared up at the mattress above her, her hands clenched beneath her blanket. Her body felt too small to contain the pounding of her heart. Every creak of the floorboards outside their room, every groan of the shack settling in the heat made her flinch.

Above her, Mark's breathing was slow and steady-but she knew it was forced. She could feel it in the tight stillness of the bed frame, in the faint rustle of his arm adjusting as he strained to listen.

He wasn't asleep.

How could he be?

No one could sleep when monsters paced the halls.

From their bed, they could hear Hattie crying.

Soft, broken sobs that bled through the thin walls like a haunting.

"I'm sorry... I'm so sorry..."

Her words barely lifted above a whisper, but they sliced through the silence like glass. Sarah squeezed her eyes shut, trying to block out the sound, but the echoes filled her head anyway.

She pictured her mother crumpled on the floor of the living room, knees tucked to her chest, rocking like she could undo the damage.

"I didn't mean for this to happen..."

But it did.

It always did.

Sarah's breath came shaky and shallow. No matter how hard she tried, she couldn't pretend everything would go back to normal. There was no normal here.

"She's crying again," Sarah whispered, voice barely audible over the hum of the cicadas outside.

Mark didn't answer at first. Above her, the bunk creaked faintly as he shifted, his silence thick with tension. She couldn't see him, but she could feel it in the stillness-the way even the air seemed to hold its breath.

"She always cries now," he muttered finally, his voice flat. Cold. "But she doesn't do anything to stop it."

There was anger in his voice-but underneath, there was something else.

Hurt.

Mark wasn't just mad.

He was scared.

111

Sarah turned toward him, their arms pressed tight together beneath the thin blanket. "We'll be okay, Mark," she whispered, even though the words felt hollow. Even though she wasn't sure she believed them anymore.

Mark didn't answer. He just shifted slightly above her, then whispered, "I won't let anything happen to you," he breathed after a moment, his words barely more than a tremble.

"I promise."

Sarah clung to that promise like a lifeline, even though she knew Mark couldn't really stop what was coming.

But she needed to believe he could.

Time crawled. The minutes stretched on endlessly, each one dragging like it was being pulled through mud. The night outside was thick with heat, but inside the shack, the air felt frozen, heavy with dread.

Steve was still out there-somewhere in the kitchen-his boots thudding across the cracked tiles, back and forth, back and forth. The scent of cheap whiskey and sweat drifted down the hall, thick and nauseating.

He hadn't gone to bed.

And that scared Sarah more than anything.

When Steve stayed awake, bad things happened.

Mark and Sarah stayed as still as possible beneath their thin blanket, their bodies tense and ready. Waiting for the sound of his steps coming closer. Waiting for the creak of the door.

Sarah squeezed her eyes shut.

"Please don't come back here," she prayed silently.

But the tension in the shack pressed down on them like a hand around their throats, squeezing tighter with every second.

Sarah tried to stay awake. She fought the pull of sleep with everything she had, but exhaustion was winning. Her eyelids drooped, her head bobbing softly against the pillow.

Until the footsteps came.

Heavy. Slow.

Coming closer.

Her eyes snapped open, her heart hammering so hard she felt it in her throat.

"Mark…" she whispered, shaking him gently.

His eyes flew open, wide and alert. He'd heard them too.

The footsteps stopped. Right outside their doorway that held no door.

Sarah's breath caught. Her hand latched onto Mark's arm, squeezing until her fingers ached.

They held their breath.

And waited.

Steve's large shadow fell across the doorway.

Sarah felt her entire body go cold. Ice prickled beneath her skin.

But then…

He stopped.

Silence.

Steve's heavy breathing lingering in the darkness, the sound low and ragged. She could feel the rage simmering-quiet but ready.

After what felt like forever, the footsteps moved away. Slow. Deliberate.

Back toward the living room.

Sarah let out a shuddering breath, but she didn't relax.

Neither did Mark.

They heard her then-Hattie's voice, small and strained.

"Steve… please. Come to bed."

Her words were slurred, heavy with exhaustion and fear.

"Shut up, Hattie," Steve snapped.

Sarah's grip tightened on the edge of her blanket. She silently begged her mother not to make things worse.

"Please," Hattie murmured again. "Just... come to bed."

There was a long pause, thick with tension.

Then finally-

"Fine."

The creak of the mattress as Steve sat down was the only sound left. The air in the shack seemed to sag under the weight of it.

But Sarah couldn't relax.

Even after the shack grew quiet, even after Steve's breathing slowed to the deep rhythm of sleep, Sarah couldn't let go of the fear.

It clung to her skin. Settled in her chest like a stone.

Mark's arm hung down from the top bunk. Sarah held it as a lone source of comfort in the abyss.

Neither of them believed it was really over.

Because it wasn't.

The night dragged on and on, stretching so long it felt like it would never end. Even when the first pale light of dawn seeped through the cracks in the walls, painting thin gold lines across the floor, Sarah felt no relief.

She lay there, wide-eyed, waiting for the next sound. The next storm.

The monsters were still there.

And nothing felt safe anymore.

Chapter 27

Several weeks had passed since that night.

The night the gun had fired.

The night the shack's walls had swallowed Hattie's screams whole.

But nobody spoke of it again.

The grown-ups exchanged a few hushed words behind closed doors, but whatever had been said was buried just as quickly. No questions. No explanations. Just silence. And Sarah, like everyone else, tucked the memory away behind thick walls of denial-locking it deep where it couldn't touch her when the sun was shining.

Life returned to whatever passed for normal in the shack. The air hung heavy with smoke and tension. The floors stayed littered with crushed beer cans and muddy footprints. And the quiet between the violence was the only peace they knew.

Until the day Steve stood in the kitchen, his voice slick with something that made Sarah's skin prickle.

"My boy's comin' to stay for a while," he announced, grinning as if this were good news.

Sarah froze, the spoon in her hand dripping milk onto the table.

The way Steve said it, though-too casual, too rehearsed-sent a chill through her. His smile didn't reach his eyes. His voice carried that edge, the one that made the hairs on the back of her neck stand up.

Like this wasn't just a visit. Like he'd already decided where this was going.

Something was about to change.

And not for the better.

The days before Evan's arrival were spent rearranging the shack. Steve barked orders, made Sarah and Mark move things around to "make room." The brown plaid love seat with solid brown cushions was shoved against the wall in the wide hallway that led through the front door, past the living room to the kitchen.

Sarah stood in the corner, arms crossed, watching as their small space got even smaller. Her chest tightened. Another body. Another stranger who'd take up air in this place where there was barely enough to breathe.

And then-Randy showed up.

Sarah lit up the second she saw him. He wasn't a boy anymore. Randy stood taller than she remembered-broad-shouldered, hands rough from turning wrenches all day. His patched jeans were stained with motor oil, the faint scent of grease and gasoline clinging to him like armor. He had the patchy start of a beard-uneven and unkempt, like he hadn't shaved in days but couldn't grow much to begin with, his eyes shadowed with something too heavy for someone his age.

But when he hugged her, the tension in her chest loosened. Just for a minute.

He tossed the football with Mark in the yard, pretending-for their sake-that the world hadn't turned into a cage. But Sarah could see the way he glanced toward the shack, the way his jaw tightened when he noticed how frail they had become. The way his eyes followed the door, as if expecting Steve to come slithering back at any second.

Sometimes Steve *did* catch Randy during his visits, always asking

116

for something under the guise of friendliness.

"You mind takin' a look at my truck?" Steve would clap him on the back like they were brothers.

Randy's eyes would narrow, his hands curling into fists at his sides. But Steve always knew how to twist the screws.

"Well, unless you don't want to..." Steve would sneer. "I'm sure you got other places to be. Don't gotta come see the kids."

And Randy-he'd bite his tongue, glance back at Sarah and Mark standing quietly by the window, and surrender. A few hours later, he'd be under the hood, hands black with grease, while Steve leaned back in his chair like a king watching his servant.

His only payment? A crumpled bag of weed thrown his way.

But this time-Steve was gone.

And Randy had something to say.

After tossing the football with Mark until the sun started to dip, Randy came inside. Hattie sat at the kitchen table, a cigarette burning low between her fingers, her eyes sunken and distant. The shack was thick with the stink of nicotine and stale beer.

Randy pulled out a chair, the scrape of wood against linoleum louder than it should've been. Sarah hovered in the doorway, pretending to clean, but her ears strained for every word.

"Why are you doing this to Mark and Sarah?" Randy's voice was tight, the frustration riding high in his throat.

Hattie took a drag from her cigarette, eyes flickering but not meeting his. "I'm not doing anything."

"Yeah, you are," he shot back. "You're lettin' Steve do whatever the hell he wants."

Hattie's arms folded across her chest, her defenses rising. "Steve's a good man. Strict, maybe. But the kids need that."

"No, Mom." Randy leaned forward, the muscles in his jaw working like he was holding back a scream. "He's not strict. He's an abuser. You know what he did to Bill. You know what he does to you. And you're lettin' him hurt them too."

"Don't talk to me like that," she snapped, but her voice was brittle.

Randy's tone softened, but the pain in it was sharper than ever. "You're scared to be alone. I get that. But you're lettin' him tear this family apart just so you don't have to wake up by yourself."

Hattie's eyes dropped to the table, the cigarette burning down between her fingers.

"It's for my own good," she mumbled. "He loves me."

Randy pushed back from the table, his chair scraping the floor. "Love doesn't make you a prisoner."

He stood, towering over her, his hands balled into fists. "Dad would never do this to you."

Her lips trembled, but she didn't speak.

He waited. Hoping. But there was only silence.

Randy's jaw clenched, and he turned away. Sarah followed him to the door, watching as he swung a leg over his motorcycle, the engine roaring to life like thunder in the quiet evening.

He didn't look back.

That night, Sarah found Hattie in the kitchen, slumped in her chair, a fresh beer in her hand, staring blankly out the smudged window. The moonlight made her look older, smaller-like the weight of everything had finally folded her in on herself.

Sarah stood in the doorway, her voice caught in her throat.

"Oh, Mom..." she whispered.

But Hattie didn't hear her.

Didn't move.

Just sat there-trapped in a world where the walls kept closing in, and she wouldn't lift a hand to stop it.

And outside, somewhere in the distance, Sarah imagined the sound of Randy's motorcycle fading into the night.

The last bit of hope driving away.

Chapter 28

The night Evan arrived, the air inside the shack thickened.

It was more than just the humidity pressing through the cracked windows—it was something heavier, something that settled in the bones. Like the house itself could sense the shape of what was coming.

Sarah felt it.

Even before the door creaked open, even before Steve's boots pounded against the cold concrete slab, she felt the change. The way the walls seemed to lean closer, the way the quiet turned brittle.

Steve stumbled through the front door, the stench of whiskey clinging to him like a second skin. His shirt clung damp to his broad frame, and his eyes—glassier than usual—scanned the room like searchlights sweeping for prey.

"Hattie," he slurred, his voice low but sharp enough to cut. "Why the hell are they still up? They've got school tomorrow."

Mark and Sarah didn't wait for the second warning. They knew the signs—the crack in his voice, the twitch in his jaw, the way his shoulders squared like a loaded gun.

Without a word, they gathered their books and drifted toward the hallway like shadows trying not to be seen.

But Steve's voice followed them.

"Hey. Hold it."

They froze mid-step, breath catching.

When they turned back, they saw him—Steve's thick hand gripping the shoulder of a boy about Mark's age. The boy stood stiff, red-faced, his clothes wrinkled from the long ride. His eyes didn't rise past the floor.

"This here's Evan," Steve announced, nudging the boy forward like he was showing off a prize steer at the county fair. "Say hi, Evan."

The boy mumbled something that might've been a greeting, his gaze flickering up and then away. His face was familiar in the worst way—a near-clone of Steve, down to the square jaw and the way his mouth pressed into a hard line like he'd learned to keep everything inside.

"My boy," Steve said, pride coating the words like grease. "Already told him about y'all. Don't need to repeat anything."

The warning hung there.

Mark and Sarah exchanged a glance—quick, tight—and mumbled "Hi" before slipping down the hallway and out of reach.

Sarah wasn't surprised when Steve started barking orders.

"The boy needs a proper bed," he snapped. "Can't have him sleepin' out here like some stray."

His arm swept toward the small back room—toward *her* bed.

"Sarah, you'll be sleeping on that loveseat."

No one asked for how long.

No one dared.

Mark kept his head down. Hattie didn't argue.

And just like that, Sarah's place in the world shrank a little more.

That night, she curled up on the battered loveseat in the hallway, her knees pulled tight against her chest, a thin blanket draped over her like it could shield her from the cold that seeped through the cracks in the walls. The overhead light in the kitchen buzzed faintly, casting flickering shadows along the wood-paneled hallway.

She tried to close her eyes, but the fight in the kitchen began before she even drifted.

"This? This is what you're servin' me?"

Steve's voice rose sharp and mean, slicing through the thin walls like a blade.

"Steve, I—"

"My boy's here sleepin', and you're bangin' around like you're workin' in a damn truck stop? And this?"—the clatter of a dish against the counter—"You thought warmed-up food was fine?"

The crack of a bottle. The sharp smack of a slap. Hattie's soft scream muffled behind her hand.

Sarah froze beneath her thin blanket, heart pounding. On the other side of the kitchen, Mark sat upright in the dark, his fists clenched, his jaw set hard.

Evan didn't make a sound.

The weeks that followed bled together.

Steve strutted through the shack like a rooster, puffed up with pride, parading Evan like a trophy. Always bragging. Always comparing.

"That boy's stronger than you'll ever be," he sneered at Mark, his gaze lingering too long. "More respect in his little finger than some of you got in your whole damn body."

Mark bit his tongue until it bled.

Sarah stayed on the loveseat.

Night after night, her back ached against the lumpy cushions, her knees drawn up to keep out the draft that curled beneath the door. Steve made sure she didn't forget where she belonged.

"You should be grateful," he chuckled once, tossing her a scratchy wool blanket. "That couch is good enough for you, some kids don't have that much."

She didn't answer.

Evan never offered the bed back. Never once asked if she was okay. But Sarah didn't blame him.

It was easier to survive when you stayed quiet.

Late one night, when the house creaked with the weight of all it held, Sarah heard Steve's voice in the kitchen.

"That boy's gonna be just like me," he bragged, the slur in his words softening nothing. "You watch."

And Sarah—lying curled on the loveseat, staring into the dark—felt her stomach twist.

Because she already knew what men like Steve could become.

And the thought of Evan becoming a reflection of that—

That made her sick to her stomach.

Chapter 29

The morning crept in colder than the last, the gray light seeping through the thin curtains like a quiet warning. Sarah stirred beneath her threadbare blanket, the ache in her back sharper than usual, her small body twisted uncomfortably on the battered loveseat in the hallway.

"Sarah, get up."

Mark's voice came soft but urgent, a hush beneath the stillness.

"We're gonna miss the bus."

She blinked, disoriented. The cold bit at her cheeks, stung the tip of her nose. Her legs were tangled in the thin blanket, her body stiff from another night spent curled too small in a space that was never meant for sleeping.

Her eyes drifted toward the bedroom door left cracked open just enough to see Evan, still sound asleep in her bed. The rise and fall of his chest was slow, steady—unbothered. School didn't seem to exist in his world.

No one had come to wake them. No clatter of pots in the kitchen, no sluggish shuffle of Hattie's feet across the warped floorboards. Just silence, thick and hollow.

Mark was already pulling on his jacket, his backpack slung over one shoulder. His breath came in quick puffs, visible in the cold air that crept through the thin walls.

"Come on!" he hissed, waving her to follow.

Sarah scrambled to her feet, heart racing. She pulled on yesterday's jeans and a wrinkled sweater in a hurry, her fingers fumbling with the buttons. The cold seeped into her skin as she stuffed her feet into her worn sneakers, grabbing her coat from the floor.

They slipped out the door, their sneakers crunching over frost-covered gravel. The chill snapped at their heels as they raced the sun, the sky still heavy with morning mist.

The bus's engine roared to life just as they reached the end of the long, winding drive. Mark waved frantically, his arms cutting through the haze, and the driver caught sight of them at the last second, brakes squealing.

Sarah stumbled up the steps behind him, her breath ragged, her heart pounding from more than just the run.

"Morning," she gasped, collapsing onto the cracked vinyl seat beside Mark.

"I wonder why Mom didn't wake us up," she whispered, her fingers trembling as she smoothed her jeans.

Mark shrugged without looking at her.

"I wonder why *he's* still asleep."

Sarah glanced out the window, the frost blurring the passing trees. "Maybe he doesn't have school," she murmured. But she didn't care. For a few precious hours, they were away from the shack.

Away from Steve.

And that was enough.

Days slipped into weeks, and Evan became another fixture in their house. Quiet. Watchful. Not cruel—but not a friend, either. He trailed after Mark like a stray dog, hovering just close enough to observe, never far enough to ignore.

Sarah didn't mind.

Distance was easier. Safer.

But Steve noticed everything.

One afternoon, as the sun dipped low and the shadows stretched long across the gravel yard, Steve swaggered in. His boots clomped hard against the floor, the stink of stale beer trailing him like a second skin.

"Get cleaned up," he barked, his voice sharp as the snap of a whip. "Takin' y'all to get toys."

Mark and Sarah exchanged glances, confusion knitting their brows.

"Toys?" Mark echoed, wary.

"Yes, toys!" Steve spat, his lips curling like the word itself insulted him. "Now move. Or me and Evan'll go without you."

It was a show.

A performance for Evan.

Steve puffed his chest, slapped the boy on the back, grinning that hard, hollow grin that never touched his eyes. He was playing the role of father—provider, protector—but Sarah could see through it. Could feel the weight of the act pressing down on them all.

For a brief, disorienting moment, she saw something human flicker across Steve's face. Pride. The kind that looked almost real. Like, in some other life, he might have been someone else.

But that flicker died fast.

The trip was nothing more than a storm waiting to break.

Grumbled complaints.

Tight smiles.

Thinly veiled threats.

Sarah lingered too long in the toy aisle, staring at a doll she couldn't afford to want.

"You think I've got all day?" Steve snapped, his breath hot on her neck. "Pick something and move."

Her hands trembled as she grabbed the cheapest plastic doll on the shelf, its smile too wide, its eyes too bright. She hugged it to her chest, swallowing back the lump in her throat.

The ride home was silent.

Evan stayed until the first snow of winter break. One morning, without warning, he was gone. No goodbyes. No explanations. Just an empty bed and the scent of his absence clinging to the air.

Sarah dragged her pillow and blanket back into the room she shared with Mark, reclaiming the thread bare mattress on the bottom bunk that had never really stopped being hers. But it felt different beneath her now. Stiffer. Hard in places that used to be soft.

The ceiling tiles hadn't changed—the same crack ran through the plaster overhead, the same shadows stretched across the walls—but something in the air had shifted.

She curled in the same corner of the bed, knees tucked tight, staring at the bottom of Mark's bunk long after the shack went quiet.

She should have felt relief.

But the silence was heavier now.

The kind that pressed against your ribs and made it hard to breathe.

The house wasn't safer.

Not really.

Not anymore.

Not ever.

Chapter 30

The winter bled away in gray streaks, and summer crept in like an unwanted guest, pressing heat into every crack of the shack. Evan returned with the season, his presence changing the air the moment he stepped through the door. It was subtle at first—the puffed-up pride in Steve's voice when he introduced Evan, his "real son." But Mark felt it. In every glance. In every word left unsaid.

He was not Steve's son.

No one needed to tell him. It was in the way Steve barely looked at him unless something was wrong. Mark had always been the scapegoat, but with Evan back, it got worse. Steve doted on Evan. Took him fishing, bought him snacks, let him sleep in while Mark stacked firewood and tended to the three pit bulls out back. Evan got to be the golden boy. Mark got the blame.

One afternoon, Mark and Sarah escaped into the woods beside the shack, their patch of freedom tucked away in the overgrowth. Mitch and Marty, Steve's nephews, were there too, huddled around a pile of baseball cards under the lean-to they had built from fallen limbs and scrap boards. It wasn't much, but it was theirs.

The sound of footsteps on the trail made Mark stiffen. Evan appeared, hands in his pockets, a smug grin stretched across his face.

"I've got a secret," Evan said, his eyes locked on Mark.

Mark narrowed his eyes, tired of the games. "What?"

"I'm not supposed to tell you," Evan taunted, grinning wider. "Dad told me not to."

Mark turned back to the cards, but his fists clenched. "Then don't."

Evan circled closer, letting the words drip like poison. "It's about your mom..."

Mark stood. His pulse thudded in his ears.

Evan took a step back, but his smirk never wavered. "He said he's only using your mom. For her check. Doesn't care about her. Or you."

The words landed like a punch. Mark's breath caught, rage clawing its way up from his chest. Before Evan could flinch, Mark lunged, tackling him to the ground. His fists flew, striking Evan again and again until his face turned red and streaked with tears.

"Tell me!" Mark shouted. "Tell me what else he said!"

Evan squirmed, his voice cracking. "That's it! That's all he said!"

After Mitch and Marty pulled him off, Mark stood, shaking, staring down at Evan like he was something he could break. Then, without a word, he turned and stormed back toward the shack.

Hattie was on the phone when Mark barreled inside, his face flushed, his hands trembling. She hung up immediately, sensing the storm behind his eyes.

"Mark? What's going on?"

He told her.

Her face drained of color. She sat down hard at the table, staring at nothing.

"I'll handle it," she whispered, waving him away.

Mark turned toward the door, but Steve's truck rattled up the gravel drive before he reached it. His stomach twisted, dread pooling in his gut.

Steve stormed through the door. Minutes later,

"Mark! Evan!"

The boys scrambled into the living room, their heads bowed. Steve slapped the backs of their heads in one swift motion.

"What the hell is this shit you're spreading?"

"Evan told me!" Mark shot back, his voice cracking. "Told me you're just using Mom!"

Steve's eyes narrowed, dark and dangerous. "That's what you get for listening to people who don't know shit. You upset your mother."

Mark turned to Hattie, guilt heavy on his chest. "I'm sorry, Mom."

Steve smirked, his grip easing. "Apologize to me, too."

Mark swallowed hard. "Sorry."

Steve waved them off. "Go outside."

As they turned to leave, Mark heard Steve's voice twist sharp, turning on Evan.

That night, as if nothing had happened, Steve threw a party. The usual crowd. Smoke, laughter, grilled meat, and cheap beer. Mark watched from the shadows, his anger simmering just beneath the surface.

After most of the guests left, Steve shook Mark and Evan awake.

"C'mon. Get dressed. We're goin' fishin'."

Mark blinked, surprised. Maybe Steve wanted to make peace.

They drove for miles, the headlights cutting through the darkness. Mark asked where they were going. Steve didn't answer.

Finally, Steve killed the engine on a desolate stretch of road.

"Get out," he ordered.

Mark's heart hammered. "Wh—what?"

"Get. Out."

Mark climbed out, the gravel crunching under his shoes. Steve peeled away, the truck disappearing into the night.

Mark stood frozen, panic rising. Then, headlights reappeared, bearing down on him.

Steve wasn't slowing down.

Mark dove to the side, scraping his hands on the gravel as the truck skidded to a stop.

Steve climbed out, looming over him. "You ever run your mouth again, you won't come back. Now get up on this road and run."

Mark hesitated, but Steve lifted the pistol from the seat, his wrist twisting it with the barrel pointed upward.

"RUN!"

Mark ran. His legs burned, his lungs heaved, but he ran. Because it was all he could do.

And every step, every desperate breath, he thought only one thing: I need my dad.

Chapter 31

The pickup idled on the gravel shoulder, its headlights carving a narrow tunnel through the Kentucky dark. Dust hung in the beams like smoke, swirling with every shift of the truck's weight. Mark's lungs burned, each ragged breath scraping his throat raw as the engine rumbled low and steady, indifferent.

The night felt endless.

Out there, in the hollow stillness of the road, Mark stood frozen beneath the glare of the headlights, his legs trembling from miles of running. His feet throbbed, torn and blistered, raw skin clinging to the insides of his shoes. Every step had been agony, each breath a sharp reminder that he'd been left to fend for himself.

Finally, the passenger door creaked open.

Evan leaned across from the middle of the seat, his thin face pale and drawn in the sickly glow of the dashboard lights.

"Hurry—get in," Evan whispered, voice quivering with something between guilt and fear.

Mark's body moved before his mind caught up. He hauled himself into the cab, sweat and dust streaking his face, his damp T-shirt clinging to his ribs. He slid onto the cracked vinyl seat, pressing close enough to Evan that their shoulders touched. The door clicked shut behind him like a trap.

Steve sat behind the wheel, hands loose on the steering wheel, eyes locked on the black ribbon of road ahead. His fingers drummed out an erratic rhythm that filled the cab with something sharp, something dangerous. The scent of sweat, smoke, and beer barely cut through the tension.

Neither boy spoke.

The truck lurched forward, tires crunching the gravel beneath them, spitting stones into the dark.

Steve's voice cut through the silence. Flat. Bored. Like they'd just finished a chore.

"You tell anyone about tonight—anyone—and next time I won't stop."

Mark swallowed hard, throat burning. He couldn't look away from the dashboard, the flickering glow of the speedometer. "Yes, sir," he rasped.

Evan echoed him, softer. "Yes, sir."

Steve gave a curt nod, as if that settled it, and turned up the radio. Grainy country static swallowed the cab, the singer's voice lost beneath the crackle. The tires hummed against the road, steady and merciless.

Neither boy dared speak again. Mark cradled his blistered feet under the dash, every throb a reminder of how close he'd come to not coming home. Evan sat stiff and silent, guilt flickering across his face whenever Steve wasn't looking.

Mark saw it.

But guilt wasn't enough to undo the night.

The shack surfaced from the predawn gloom, hunched against the horizon like something ashamed to be seen. The porch bulb flickered weakly, casting shadows that stretched too far, too thin. Only the bathroom light glowed inside, a lone beacon in the dark.

Steve killed the engine and shoved the door open. Gravel crunched beneath his boots as he nudged the boys forward.

"Shower," he muttered. "Both of you. Scrub the road off."

Mark's legs barely worked. His feet felt like fire. But he moved, each step dragging him through the sagging doorway, down the musty hallway, past a barely sleeping Sarah. Evan hovered behind him, glancing back at Steve as though afraid he'd change his mind.

The bathroom was small, barely big enough to turn around in. Rust clung to the edges of the sink, and the tub's enamel was cracked and yellowed.

Mark slumped onto the edge of the tub and peeled off his socks, wincing as the fabric stuck to the blisters beneath. Blood smeared across his heels. Evan hovered in the doorway, his eyes wide at the sight of Mark's torn feet.

"Man..." Evan whispered, voice cracking. "I'm sorry."

Mark didn't answer. Couldn't. His hands trembled as he twisted the faucet, the pipes groaning in protest. Rust-tinged water hissed from the spout, barely warm. The two boys traded places, each taking their turn beneath the tepid stream. First Mark, scrubbing the dust and sweat from his raw skin, biting his lip to keep from crying out as the water stung like needles. Then Evan, silent as he rinsed away the road.

Neither spoke.

The only sound was the hiss of water, the squeak of the faucet turning, the distant murmur of Steve's voice—half-drunk, half-muttering to himself in the living room.

Mark's body ached-every muscle, every blister screaming-but it was nothing compared to the weight inside his chest. He lay on his side, staring at the cracked ceiling, tracing the jagged lines like they held the answer to everything.

Steve's voice still echoed in his skull.

Next time, I won't stop.

He swallowed hard, pressing his face into the pillow, burying the tears that wanted to come. He couldn't let them out. Not here. Not now.

Sleep crept in slowly, wrapping around the edges of his pain like smoke. His blistered feet throbbed with every heartbeat. His fists clenched beneath the blanket.

But the fear stayed.

It always stayed.

And in the hours before dawn, while the birds outside began to sing, Mark dreamed of running.

But this time, no one came back for him.

Chapter 32

After nearly a year of building up his drug business—buying and selling pot, forging connections, weaving his web of whispers and shadows—Steve finally brought them to what he called *"a real home."*

But nothing about it felt real.

From the outside, the house sat nestled in the rolling Kentucky countryside, its mustard-yellow siding faded beneath the sloped metal roof. A gravel driveway snaked down from the road that curled like a lazy river through fields dotted with wildflowers and weeds. But beneath the surface, beneath the illusion, the truth sat waiting.

It was a double-wide trailer.

A shell of wood and siding built around it—thin walls dressed up to mimic permanence. Like if it just looked the part, it could somehow *become* something more. But it wasn't. Not really.

It sat a half mile from the nearest paved street, hidden beneath the shade of old oak trees, surrounded by ten acres of land that rolled like the harsh swell of ocean waves. Behind the house, a narrow creek trickled softly, its banks heavy with brush and broken limbs. Beyond the creek loomed a sagging red barn, ribs showing through the weathered slats, leaning like it was tired of standing.

There were fields, too. Eight cows swayed their tails lazily at flies, grazing beneath the wide-open sky. A barbed-wire fence circled the acre-wide garden Steve had plotted off himself, straight lines cut into the earth, ready for planting.

For the first time in a long time, there was space to breathe.

The air smelled different here—damp dirt, fresh grass, and manure. It clung to their clothes, mingling with the ever-present smoke of Hattie's Winstons and Steve's Camels. Cigarette smoke drifted like ghosts through every room of the house, curling around the light fixtures, staining the ceiling and television screen yellow.

Inside, it was dim, like the sun couldn't quite make it through the heavy curtains or the dark wood paneling that lined every wall. The carpet was thick and brown, worn threadbare in places. Mismatched floral sofas sagged across from one another in the living room, their cushions flattened from years of bodies sinking into them. A battered recliner slouched in between them. A green floral hand-me-down chair sat in front of the corner near the hallway—a spot Mark would come to know intimately. Across from the front door, a half wall revealed the coat closet, with a low bookshelf beneath it cluttered with paperbacks, stray lighters, and overflowing ashtrays.

But there was something else here, too. Something that felt... quiet.

For the first time in as long as they could remember, Steve wasn't drinking.

He promised this place would be different. And for two whole months, it was.

Steve stayed sober. He mowed the wild grass that had swallowed the yard. He hammered the fence posts back into place, his broad back bent beneath the sun. He joked with the kids. Called Mark *champ*. Gave Sarah rides in the back of the old pickup when they went into town.

He talked about building something here. Starting over. *Making the land work for them.*

And for a while, they believed him.

Sarah watched him kneel in the garden, sifting the soil between his fingers like he knew what he was doing. She watched the way his eyes scanned the horizon, like he could see a future out there.

Mark, cautious but curious, explored the barn and the woods behind it. He mapped the trails like they were his to claim, finding the places where the deer slipped through the brush, where the creek bent sharp beneath the willows.

For a moment, they allowed themselves to believe. To imagine.

At school, Sarah made friends. The other girls didn't know who she was yet—didn't know about the shack, the nights spent curled on the loveseat, the fear that haunted her footsteps. She could be anyone here. Anyone she wanted.

Some nights, laughter echoed from the house. Hattie danced barefoot in the kitchen, spinning slow circles beneath the dim light, her hair falling in loose waves across her face. Steve stood outside by the shed, flipping burgers on the grill, smoke curling into the twilight while the kids ran wild across the fields, chasing fireflies beneath the fading sun.

It felt like a beginning.

Like maybe this time, things would be different.

Maybe this time, *they* would be different.

But beginnings, Sarah knew, never lasted long in her world. They cracked and splintered, gave way beneath the weight of reality.

Still, for those few fragile weeks, they held onto hope.

And hope—even the fragile kind—felt like magic.

Chapter 33

It was summer 1983.

The kind of summer that changes everything. The kind that creeps in slow and heavy, pressing down on your skin until you can't tell where the heat ends and you begin. The kind of summer when you stop being a child, whether you're ready or not. When the world sharpens at the edges, and you start seeing too much.

It was before Evan came back. Before the worst of it.

But the air was already shifting.

The house never stayed quiet for long. Not in the summers.

Weekends were the worst. Steve's friends and relatives would roll up in dented pickups and rust-bitten sedans, doors slamming like gunshots. They came heavy-handed—arms full of cheap beer, bottles of whiskey stuffed under their arms, pockets clinking with bad ideas. They brought their girlfriends, their kids, their fists full of smokes and half-told stories that never ended well.

They drank before the sun dipped low, and they didn't stop until the sky turned soft with morning. The house—just two bedrooms— somehow held them all. Bodies sprawled across couches, slumped in chairs, passed out on the threadbare carpet, sweat, dust, and smoke curling through every room like mold.

Steve barked orders, the king of his crumbling castle.

Hattie played hostess, pouring drinks with a painted-on smile, pretending not to see when Steve's mood turned mean.

And Sarah and Mark?

They became shadows. Ghosts in their own home.

They stepped over legs, dodged glassy-eyed stares, slipped through the cracks like mice. Barefoot. Silent.

That summer, the work never ended.

The garden stretched nearly an acre—row after row of corn, beans, tomatoes, cucumbers, squash. A kingdom of labor under the brutal Kentucky sun.

Every morning began early, with Steve barking orders. Every chore carried the weight of a threat.

No gloves. No water until the job was done. No shade, except the thin mercy offered by the clouds that rarely lingered. Their fingers calloused and cracked from pulling weeds and stacking wood. Their backs bent until they ached. Their skin turned red, blistered, peeling and raw.

Lunch was a gamble. Sometimes there was food. Sometimes they worked straight through, the hunger gnawing at their stomachs, sharpening their edges.

Mitch and Marty, Steve's nephews, rarely helped. They stayed inside, waiting for the work to end. And when it did, when Steve finally grunted that they could "get lost," the kids scattered like leaves.

And Mark and Sarah ran.

Ran toward the only place that felt like theirs.

Past the creek, up the hill just below the garden, there was a pond. Oval shaped, deep green, perfect. Its cool, dark water wrapped around them like safety.

Mark dove first, his splash breaking the stillness, his laughter echoing across the fields. Sarah waded in slower, letting the mud squish between her toes, the water rising to swallow her heat-flushed skin.

In that pond, the world melted away.

No Steve. No chores. No fear.

Just water.

Just freedom.

Farther into the woods, there was the vine swing.

Thick and rough, it hung from the tallest tree, swaying just above the edge of the hill. They called it *the flying vine.* Their secret escape.

One by one, they lined up on the flat rock that jutted over the drop, gripping the vine with calloused hands. Then came the run—the leap—the moment their feet left the earth.

And for a few precious seconds, they flew.

Weightless. Untouchable. Free.

Their laughter soared higher than the trees, echoing through the woods, defiant. For those moments, they were kids again.

Sometimes Mitch and Marty joined them. Sometimes the kids of Steve's friends, and sometimes Evan. They carved their names into tree trunks, swapped ghost stories, dared each other to jump higher, swing farther.

For a while, it felt like a normal summer.

But laughter never lasted long under Steve's roof.

He didn't like joy unless it belonged to him.

Didn't like laughter he couldn't control.

Sarah knew that. Mark did too.

Even in the brightest moments, the storm was always there—rumbling low, just beneath the surface, waiting for its chance to break.

Looking back, Sarah would remember that summer with a strange ache.

Not just for the joy they squeezed from it—but for the knowing.

For the quiet dread that settled in the bones when you realized magic was borrowed. That no matter how high you flew, the ground was waiting.

The garden would keep growing. The sun would keep shining.

But there, just beyond the trees, the storm waited.

And when it came, no vine swing in the world could carry them far enough to escape it.

Chapter 34

That fall, the air grew thin.

Not just with the season changing, but inside Sarah too.

She sat cross-legged on the floor, her back pressed hard against the wooden frame of the bed, a spiral notebook sprawled across her lap. The thin mattress above creaked as Mark shifted, getting ready to head outside.

"What are you doing?" His voice cracked the silence.

"Studying." She flipped to the next page, tracing the neat diagrams she'd drawn earlier—charts of the water cycle, sketches of plant cells. Science. She loved science.

"For a test?" Mark sounded confused, like the idea of studying without a reason made no sense.

"No." She barely looked up. Her hair slipped from around her ear and into her eyes, long and unruly, but she pushed it back and kept reading.

Mark shrugged, already halfway to the door. "Nerd."

She didn't react. Couldn't.

"I'm going out with the dogs," he called, letting the screen door slap shut behind him.

Only then did she breathe again.

Her eyes scanned the familiar words, the diagrams she'd traced a hundred times before. She wasn't learning anything new. She wasn't even reading.

She was hiding.

Science was the only place where the world made sense.

If you followed the rules, you got answers.

If you measured right, mixed right, you got results.

There was safety in predictability.

And Sarah needed predictable.

Steve was chaos wrapped in skin.

There were no formulas for Steve. No rules she could follow to keep him at bay. He erupted without warning, exploded for reasons no one could guess. She turned to science because it was the only thing that didn't shout at her, didn't hit her, didn't demand her fear.

And if she worked hard enough—if she stayed invisible—maybe she could disappear.

Mark wasn't like that.

Mark pushed back.

He wasn't defiant. He was just himself—sharp and bright, too full of life to hide.

But Steve hated that.

Steve hated Mark.

The report cards told the story. Cs. Ds. Occasionally, an F.

Steve never needed an excuse, but that? That was fuel.

"I don't want any dumbasses under my roof," Steve growled, snapping Mark's report card in half like a twig. "You think you can just slack off in my house?"

The punishments came quick.

The corner. Behind the green chair.

Nose kept an inch from the wall, never allowed to touch. His arms at his sides. Hours on end. No food. No bathroom. No breaks.

"Move a muscle, and I'll make it worse," Steve snarled.

If Mark scratched his nose, shifted his weight, flinched—Steve was there. A shove, a slap, a punch to the ribs.

Sarah sat in the other room, pretending not to hear.

But she heard.

Every thud, every cry swallowed down into silence.

And she hated herself for being too afraid to stop it.

Steve controlled everything.

When they ate. What they ate. How much they ate. How loud they breathed.

Breakfast was cold cereal-if there was any.

Lunch? Peanut butter sandwiches, if they were lucky.

Dinner was whatever Steve wanted.

But on occasional weekends, if Steve was in a good mood-or hungover just enough to want comfort-Hattie would fry up sausage and eggs, the kind usually reserved just for him. On those mornings, Mark and Sarah were allowed a plate too. Small portions carefully measured. But still, it felt like a feast.

Other kids had popsicles in the summer, ice cream on hot days.

They had cucumbers.

And dry toast.

The bread came in bulk from the discount bread store and was stacked in the deep freezer that hummed quietly in the corner of the dining room. Hattie would defrost a few loaves at a time, the slices soft and soggy at first, then brittle and dry once toasted.

Sarah salted hers and pretended it was something better.

But it wasn't.

It was survival.

Sarah didn't ask for much.

She didn't dream big.

She just wanted to feel normal. To belong somewhere.

But even in that house, she wasn't really there.

Mark had his friends-comic book nerds and misfits who circled around him like planets.

But Sarah?

She had her books. Her notebooks. Her diagrams and the neat, predictable rules of science. Those things wouldn't go away.

It was all she trusted.

Then came the kitten.

A neighbor girl found it first—a tiny thing, soft gray fur with green eyes too big for its head. She'd pressed it into Sarah's arms, whispering, "Keep her. She needs someone."

Sarah named her Daisy.

Although he had pit bulls for fighting, Steve didn't allow pets. Didn't allow softness.

So Sarah kept Daisy hidden in the barn, tucked behind a rusted feed bin, wrapped in rags and straw.

Every day, she snuck scraps—bits of bread, leftovers from the table and handfuls of dog food—to the barn. Daisy would purr and curl against her side, licking Sarah's fingers when she cried. The kitten was warmth. A secret. A soft place in a hard world.

Until the afternoon Steve followed her.

She didn't hear him coming.

Didn't realize he was there until his shadow fell across the stall.

"What's this?" he sneered, eyes narrowing as he crouched beside Daisy.

"My kitten." Sarah's voice was small but steady.

Steve stared at the kitten for a long moment, a cruel grin spreading slowly across his face.

"Come on," he said, scooping Daisy up with one hand. "Let's show her off."

Sarah scrambled to her feet, panic rising in her throat.

"Where are you going?"

"Just showing her off."

She followed, her heart thudding in her chest, dread settling like stone in her stomach.

Past the shed.

Down the slope behind the barn.

The pit bulls stirred before they even reached the edge of the clearing—twelve of them, chained to whiskey barrel doghouses, barking and snarling, their logging chains rattling against the dirt.

Steve stopped in front of Mae, the largest of the dogs, a blonde brindle with a white snout that trailed up between her eyes and around her neck. Her teeth were bared in a low, hungry growl.

Sarah froze.

"Don't," she whispered, her voice breaking. "Please."

But Steve didn't look at her.

He dangled the kitten by the scruff, just above Mae's snapping jaws.

"No!" she screamed, running toward him.

But it was too late.

He let go.

Mae lunged.

The world shattered.

Daisy's tiny body disappeared beneath snarling teeth and snapping jaws. It was over in seconds.

Sarah's scream ripped through the clearing.

Steve turned, and with one swift motion, backhanded her hard enough to send her sprawling into the dirt.

"Remember your place," he growled.

She didn't cry.

Didn't move.

She stared at the blood in the dirt, her breath shallow and ragged.

Mark found her there, sitting in the dust, her eyes hollow. He helped her back to the house, but she didn't say a word.

She never spoke of it again.

But she never forgot.

Because Daisy was the last soft thing she had.

And Steve killed her—just to remind Sarah that he could.

Chapter 35

The house groaned beneath the weight of bodies that Labor Day weekend in 1983—more crowded than it had ever been. It felt like the whole of Steve's bloodline had spilled out onto the land, like the earth itself couldn't hold them all.

Steve's brother Bobby rolled up first, trailing the sour tang of beer sweat and diesel fumes. Kathy followed close behind, her perfume sharp enough to sting. Their kids—Jay, sixteen, wiry and mean-eyed; Kevin, fourteen, too quiet; Angie, eight, all legs and laughter; and Becky, barely four—spilled out of the truck, chasing each other across the gravel.

Steve's sister Terry arrived next, dragging Mitch and Marty along. Mitch, fifteen, already carried himself like he owned the place; Marty, twelve, hovered close behind, never far from his older brother's shadow.

And then came the Florida boys—Brian and Mike. Steve's nephews. Brian was twenty-one, stocky and rough. Mike, just eighteen, wore the same hard scowl Steve did, like it had been handed down through the bloodline. Their mother—Steve's sister Sandy—had overdosed a few years back. That loss hovered around them like a ghost no one spoke of.

Sarah stood at the edge of the porch, Mark beside her, both of them watching as the yard filled up with strangers who shared Steve's face.

"I find it hard to believe Steve has a family like this," she muttered under her breath.

Mark narrowed his eyes, jaw tight. "I can't believe he's related to anyone."

But what unsettled them most wasn't the crowd. It was Steve.

The way he acted around them. Laughing. Joking. His voice light, his fists still. He wore a mask that almost fit—a version of himself that didn't shout, didn't shove, didn't bruise. Watching him pretend to be human was worse than the beatings.

"Doesn't today feel… almost good?" Mark asked, his voice low as they stood near the old swing set, his bare feet pressed into the sun-warmed grass.

"Good?" Sarah echoed, wary but curious.

He nodded toward the house without looking at it. "He's wrapped up with them. Not watching us."

Sarah let out a small breath, not quite a laugh, but close.

It wasn't peace—not really.

But for now, it was quiet.

And in a place like this, quiet felt like a gift you didn't question.

For one day, Steve was too busy playing king to notice them.

And in that rare pocket of freedom, Mark and Sarah carved out something that felt like joy.

They swam in the pond until their fingers pruned, chased fireflies with Mitch, Marty, Angie and Becky as the sky turned the color of burning embers. They climbed trees, swung wild from the vine, shouted into the woods just to hear their echoes come back.

It felt like summer should feel.

Like what it might feel to be normal.

For the first time in a long time, Sarah felt something warm rise up in her chest that wasn't fear.

She liked being around people that day.

The other kids. The noise. The running.

It felt like being a child again.

As the sun sank lower, painting the sky in streaks of violet and gold, the smell of grilled food crept through the yard, softening the edges of the evening.

"Hot dogs, potato salad, corn on the cob, and baked beans!" Hattie's voice floated from the kitchen window, full of a cheer that didn't sound forced for once.

Everyone lined up—Steve first, of course, plate piled high by Hattie's nervous hands. But for once, he took it without a grunt of complaint. The adults followed, then the kids, plates heavy with food that tasted like a holiday.

"Let's sit outside!" Angie chirped, her face lit up like a lantern.

They all agreed, scattering to the porch and the yard, the air cooling as stars blinked awake in the soft dusk. The fireflies danced low in the grass, laughter bubbled easy from the crowd, and for a flicker of a moment, it felt like the world might hold.

Sarah sat on the porch steps, plate balanced on her knees, the warmth of the day still clinging to her skin. She watched the others— Mitch tossing a football to Kevin, Becky chasing shadows across the yard, Jay watching.

For that one night, with bellies full and the air soft and kind, life felt almost… good.

But Sarah knew better.

Good things didn't last here.

Tomorrow would come, and with it, Steve's mask would slip.

The laughter would fade.

The bruises would return.

But for that one night, they let themselves believe.

And sometimes, pretending was enough.

Chapter 36

It started with the drinking.

It always started with the drinking.

Steve was in one of his moods—that brand of cocky, swaggering celebration that meant trouble was just waiting its turn. He pulled out the "good stuff" for the occasion, tossing cheap beer to anyone with an empty hand, the bottles cracking open like warning shots. The air inside the house thickened with usual cigarette smoke and the sour-sweet haze of pot, curling into the corners like ghosts that never left.

Laughter echoed off the wood-paneled walls. Boots scuffed the worn carpet. Jokes flew louder, looser.

Everyone was having a good time.

Everyone except Sarah.

She stood near the kitchen door, one hand on the frame, feeling the vibrations of every stomp, every slap of a beer can on the table. Her stomach knotted tighter with each laugh that rose too sharp, too fast. She'd learned to hear it—the thin edge of something mean under all that noise.

Steve was a happy drunk—at first.

When the beer flowed, he was all backslaps and stories, playing the friendly uncle, the generous host. But when the whiskey came out—that's when the real Steve stepped into the room.

Sarah heard it before she saw it.

"Go get more," Steve barked, shoving a crumpled bill toward Hattie and Kathy. His voice was slurred but his eyes—those eyes—were razor sharp.

"Bring me a fifth of Old Barton," he sneered. "None of that cheap shit."

Hattie laughed like she wasn't afraid. Kathy grabbed her purse. The screen door creaked shut behind them.

Sarah's throat tightened, the chill of dread crawling up her spine. She knew what came next. She always knew.

The storm had just begun.

The house split into factions—girls in Sarah and Mark's room, boys on the porch.

But the tension thickened like humidity before a summer storm, hanging heavy in the air.

Sarah sat on the floor, back pressed to the wall, knees hugged to her chest. Angie and Becky chattered quietly, playing Go Fish, trying to pretend everything was fine. But Sarah couldn't shake the weight pressing down on her chest.

And then—

CRASH.

The sound tore through the house.

"Shut your fuckin' mouth!" Steve roared.

"Why? What the hell you gonna do about it?" Bobby mocked.

Sarah's heart slammed against her ribs.

"Don't fuck with me, Bobby!" Steve roared, his voice splitting the air like a jagged crack in the drywall.

Another crash, this one shaking the walls. Fists. Bodies. Slamming, pounding. The sound of furniture splintering beneath the force.

Sarah flinched as a loud thud cracked against the wall behind her head. The girls froze, their eyes wide, cards slipping from their fingers.

"Oh my God," Sarah whispered, her voice shaking, her body frozen.

Then Mark's face appeared in the doorway, pale and urgent, his eyes wild.

"Hey! Out the back. Now!" He motioned fast, waving them toward the sliding glass door.

Sarah didn't argue. None of them did.

They slipped out the door like shadows, feet barely touching the grass, hearts pounding like drums in the dark.

Behind the house, over the creek. Toward the dam of the pond, just before the dirt road curved right for its final ascent to the garden.

The farther they ran, the colder the air felt—biting, sharp, slicing through the heavy heat of the day.

Angie clutched Becky's hand, tears streaming down her face. "What's happening?" she choked out.

"I don't know," Mark gasped, glancing back toward the house. The windows glowed faintly, shadows of bodies still locked in a storm of movement.

The shouting raged on. Steve. Bobby. Their voices rising, crashing, splitting the night open.

And then—

BANG.

The sound cracked the air in half.

Angie screamed. Her knees buckled, clutching Hope tighter.

Sarah hit the ground, her hands over her head, the breath knocked clean out of her lungs.

"Uncle Steve shot Dad!" Angie wailed, voice raw and broken.

Another crack of chaos. The kids scattered, panic swallowing them whole.

But Sarah couldn't move.

Her mind froze—caught somewhere between the sound of the gun and the blood she imagined blooming behind her closed eyes.

Then—

BANG.

Glass shattered behind them.

The sliding door exploded outward, shards slicing through the night like glass rain.

"Sarah, move!" Mark grabbed her arm, yanking her to her feet.

She stumbled, sobbing, "Mark... Mom..."

"No time! Go!" he shouted, pulling her forward.

They ran. Barefoot. Breathless. Up and around the dirt road and into the garden, away from the house, away from the gunfire. Away from the wreckage of whatever home had existed before.

Behind them, the house still glowed.

Still roared.

Still burned with something Sarah couldn't name.

And somewhere in the middle of that war zone, Steve stood holding the barrel of a gun.

And they—

They were just kids,

running from a battle they never should've been part of.

Because nothing—

not the food, not the laughter, not the lies—

could hide the truth:

They were never safe here.

Chapter 37

They didn't stop running until the garden rose before them like a dark, crooked monument beneath the moon. The rows of beans and tomatoes, once so familiar, now loomed like sentries in the night. Their leaves whispered in the breeze, brushing together like hands wringing in worry.

At the crest of the hill, Mark and Jay corralled the scattered group, drawing them close beneath the patchy glow of the stars. The air had turned cold, cutting through the sweat that still clung to their skin. Beneath them, the soil radiated the heat of the day, but it offered no comfort now.

"It's gonna be fine," Jay murmured, his voice thin, cracking at the edges.

No one believed him.

Sarah pulled her knees tight to her chest, hugging them so hard it hurt. The world felt too loud and too quiet all at once. Every rasp of breath, every shift of weight in the dirt felt like it echoed off the hills.

But underneath it all, she could still hear it.

The echoes of the house.

Steve's voice—exploding like thunder.

Glass breaking like bones.

Gunfire cracking through the dark.

Angie rocked on her heels, her arms wrapped around Becky like armor, but the little girl still trembled. Even the older boys— Mitch, Marty, Kevin—stood frozen, their usual bravado drained away beneath the weight of what they'd witnessed.

No one spoke. No one dared to move.

The night stretched long, carved into unbearable fragments of time.

A branch snapped in the distance.

A coyote howled.

Every sound felt sharper now, teeth bared beneath the dark.

When the boys finally ventured down to the house, their bodies stiff with fear, Sarah couldn't watch. She buried her face in her arms and waited, heart pounding with each second they didn't return.

When they came back, Jay's face was ashen. His shoulders sagged.

"It's over," he whispered. But the words felt hollow.

Becky's tiny voice trembled in the dark. "Is Daddy dead?"

Jay shook his head, slow. "No. He's okay." But there was no relief in his voice.

The night hadn't taken lives—but it had broken something. Something no one could mend.

When they crept back down to the shack, the moon lit the wreckage like a spotlight on a crime scene. The house looked hollow. Gutted.

The dining room table lay on its side, one leg snapped clean off, the splintered wood jutting out like a broken limb. Chairs were overturned, crushed beneath boot prints and shattered glass. The sliding glass door hung jagged in its frame, the breeze stirring the broken shards across the carpet like dry leaves.

The blood-red dining room carpet.

It gleamed beneath the moonlight.

Glass crunched under their bare feet, biting into the skin, but no one flinched.

Sarah's gaze caught on the upright freezer in the corner, its surface gleaming silver in the darkness, cold and impassive amid the ruin.

On the sagging sofa bed near the wood stove, Bobby and Kathy lay sprawled beneath a heap of crumpled blankets, snoring softly. The floor was littered with bodies—Mitch, Marty, Kevin—passed out, draped wherever they'd fallen, slack-jawed and oblivious.

Steve and Hattie had gone to bed.

As if none of it had ever happened.

Hattie too.

The bedroom door stood shut, sealing away whatever monsters still lingered behind it.

Sarah stood frozen in the middle of the room, fists clenched at her sides.

How?

How could they sleep?

Her jaw tightened, her body trembling with something sharp and dangerous. Rage boiled under her skin, too big for her small frame to contain.

Tiny shards bit into the bottoms of her bare feet, but she barely felt them. She moved like a ghost through the bodies, glass crunching beneath her with each step. Her heart pounded, but everything else felt far away-muted. She just kept walking. Toward the door. Toward them.

Mark's hand caught her wrist, stopping her in the doorway.

"Don't wake them up," he whispered, voice low but fierce.

His eyes—wide and knowing—met hers.

Sarah swallowed hard. Her pulse drummed in her ears.

She gave a stiff nod and let him lead her back down the hallway, her anger trailing behind her like smoke.

Their shared room—mostly untouched by the chaos, except for the bullet hole high on the wall facing the outside—waited in a hollow, uneasy stillness. The hole sat just twelve inches above Mark's pillow, a brutal reminder of how close it had come.

Mark climbed onto the top bunk without a word. Below him, Sarah lay on her mattress, arms at her sides, fingers gripping the edge of the blanket between her thumb and forefinger, eyes locked on the ceiling above.

The walls seemed thinner now.

The shadows deeper.

Her skin prickled with the weight of what they'd witnessed.

The pulse in her ears wouldn't quiet.

That rhythmic throb—louder than breath. Louder than the crickets outside.

Mark turned once, twice, trying to settle. But sleep wouldn't come.

And Sarah knew.

That night—

The gunshots, the glass, the running—

It had carved something new into her bones.

There would be no going back.

Not to safety.

Not to the illusion of it.

Not to who she'd been before the storm broke.

Something inside her had shifted.

Chapter 38

The morning after the gunfire, the house stood hollow, as if even the walls were holding their breath. Glass still littered the carpet like confetti, and the overturned table sagged in its brokenness. But Steve rose with the sun—unshaken, unbothered.

He didn't apologize. He didn't speak of the gunshots or the way fear had chased the children into the hills. Instead, he stomped through the wreckage with a hammer in hand, grumbling curses under his breath as he began to patch what he'd torn apart.

The week that followed was worse than any before.

He hammered a new sliding door back into place, the nails screaming each time they pierced the frame. He patched the cracked table leg with glue and spite. He ordered Sarah to sweep and vacuum the shattered glass, muttering about how much it all cost—how much *Hattie* had made him spend.

But something inside him had twisted too tight that night, and it didn't loosen.

Usually, after these explosions, there would be a brief calm. A sick kind of remorse that dulled the edges of his anger—for a while, at least.

But not this time.

This time, the storm never broke. It just settled deeper, festering in his bones.

And Hattie wore the bruises.

The weekend came, thick with humidity, the air pressed down like a lid on a pot ready to boil over. When Sarah caught sight of her mother, her stomach clenched.

Hattie's eyes were twin bruises—bloated, swollen, both blackened into purple shadows. One cheekbone puffed up beneath the angry blotches, and a split in her lip glistened raw.

Steve stood by the freezer, lighting a cigarette like nothing had happened.

"Look what you made me do," he sneered, the smoke curling around his smile. He watched her wince as she poured a cup of coffee, her hands trembling just enough to spill a few drops onto the counter.

No one asked what had happened. No one dared.

But Sarah could feel it—something in her mother had cracked.

The broken glass could be swept away, the door hammered back into place, but Hattie? She was done pretending.

For the first time in years, she moved with a purpose Sarah had never seen before.

She waited for the right moment.

For Steve to leave, to climb into his battered truck and rattle off down the gravel road toward whatever "business" kept him gone half a day.

As the dust settled behind him, Hattie crossed the kitchen, grabbed the stained phone off the hook, and called someone Sarah hadn't heard their name in years.

Eleanor.

Uncle Jack's ex-wife. The woman who had once shared coffee with Hattie, who had braided Sarah's hair when she was small. Eleanor wasn't loud. She wasn't fierce. But she was steady—strong in the way people get when they've weathered enough storms of their own.

The call was short. Simple.

Come get us.

Eleanor didn't ask questions.

She just came.

By the time Eleanor's car rolled into the drive, the house was quiet in that eerie way it always was after a blow-up. The air still smelled of cigarettes and something heavier—something that clung to the skin and settled deep in the lungs.

Eleanor stepped out, her face pale but determined, her hands steady even though they trembled just slightly at her sides.

She took one look at Hattie's face—the swollen eyes, the cracked lip—and something hardened behind her gentle eyes.

"Come on," she said softly, reaching for the children first.

Sarah hesitated, glancing back at the shack as if the walls might crumble the second they left. Mark stood stiff, jaw clenched, his hand brushing Sarah's shoulder. Hattie gathered the few things they could carry—bags worn thin with years of use—and followed Eleanor toward the car.

When the door shut behind them, the quiet felt heavier than any scream.

As the car bounced down the gravel road, the house grew smaller in the rearview mirror. But Sarah couldn't stop staring.

That shack had been their prison. Their cage.

And yet... leaving felt like tearing something loose inside her. Something raw. Something afraid.

Her fingers gripped the door handle, knuckles white.

Beside her, Hattie sat silent, eyes on the horizon, one hand resting on her lap like it didn't belong there.

Relief buzzed under Sarah's skin.

But beneath it—deeper—was something else.

Fear.

Because this wasn't over.

Steve wouldn't let it be over.

Sarah could feel it in her bones.

This wasn't freedom.

This was just a flicker of escape.

And flickers, she knew, could burn out fast.

Chapter 39

Steve came home to silence. The house, once filled with smoke, shouting, and the echo of his own rage, was still—too still. No Hattie. No kids. No control.

And no control meant his grip on everything—on his side business, on Hattie, on the money—was slipping.

Fast.

Panic gripped him harder than he cared to admit. The house wasn't just empty—it was hollow. The beer cans on the counter, the ashtray brimming with butts, the torn cushion on the couch—all reminders that without them, without the people he'd bent to his will, there was nothing left here but rot.

So, he did the one thing no one expected.

He picked up the phone.

The spiral-bound directory sat buried beneath stacks of past-due bills and crumpled cigarette packs. His fingers fumbled through the pages, the ink smudged, the paper stained. When he found her number, his hand hovered, shaking.

Vanessa answered on the third ring.

"Vanessa." His voice oiled itself into something almost soft. "I don't know why she'd leave. I love her. I love the kids. I've done everything I can to show them that."

There was a pause. A sharp inhale. Vanessa's voice came back like a blade.

"Really?" she snapped. "Because that's not how it looks from here."

Steve swallowed the lump in his throat, pressed harder, his desperation bleeding through.

"Just... tell me where they are. I know I've made mistakes, but I can fix it."

Another pause.

Then came Vanessa's low, mocking laugh. Cold. Merciless.

"I'd love to help you out," she said, voice dripping with venom, "but I don't know where Mom and the kids are."

Steve's mask cracked.

"You're lying!" His voice boomed through the receiver, raw and furious. "You've always been a uppity little bitch! You're hiding her from me!"

Click.

The dial tone buzzed in his ear.

But Steve wasn't done. He called again. And again. Until the phone rang hollow. Until the silence on the other end became a wall he couldn't punch through.

Vanessa took the phone off the hook and left it that way.

Eleanor kept her word.

She took Hattie and the kids in, offered them warmth, safety-a soft place to land. But her offer came with one unbending rule:

No drinking.

Eleanor was deeply religious, a southern Baptist and wouldn't bend on this.

For Hattie, that rule was a chain. Sobriety wasn't comfort. It wasn't safety. It was raw. Unnerving. And within a day, the cravings started twisting through her like vines.

She made the calls.

First to Vanessa-asking if Mark and Sarah could stay with her "just for a bit." Then, quietly, to Steve.

Mark and Sarah spent two nights at Vanessa's house in Jeffersontown. It wasn't fancy, but it smelled like lavender and soap instead of cigarettes and rot. The walls were soft colors. The nights were quiet.

They ate spaghetti at a real table. Slept through the night without the fear of doors slamming or fists flying. Vanessa put on movies, pulled out board games, tried to keep their minds busy. But her phone never stopped ringing.

Steve's number blinked on the screen over and over. Finally, Vanessa yanked the cord from the wall.

Still, by morning, they all knew what was coming.

Vanessa called Eleanor's house, asking for her mother.

Hattie was in the back bedroom, perched on the edge of the mattress, a cigarette burning down between her fingers. The ash clung long, like it was too tired to fall. She didn't turn when Vanessa's voice came through the receiver.

"Mom. Please. You're out. You don't have to go back."

Hattie's eyes stayed fixed on the wall, her voice flat and distant.

"Maybe he'll appreciate me now."

Vanessa bit back the scream rising in her throat.

"Good luck with that," she muttered, and hung up.

The next morning, Hattie stood in Eleanor's kitchen, whispering into the phone.

"If you stop being so mean…" she cooed into the receiver, the syrupy sweetness sickening. "Maybe I'll come back."

Eleanor's rule hung heavy over the house. No drinking. No exceptions.

But for Hattie, the bottle was stronger than the bruises.

Stronger than the fear.

Stronger than the offer of safety.

She chose Steve.

She chose the devil she knew.

And Steve welcomed her back like she'd never left.

When Vanessa dropped Hattie and the kids back at the house, she wasn't even allowed to walk them to the door.

Steve stood on the porch, arms crossed, daring her to get too close.

Vanessa didn't fight. Didn't plead.

She gripped the steering wheel, white-knuckled, her heart breaking, watching from the driver's seat as Sarah climbed the porch steps without looking back.

Sarah stood in the doorway, watching Vanessa pull away.

She didn't wave.

And Vanessa never turned around.

In that moment, Sarah knew:

Vanessa was done trying to save their mother.

And this time, they were truly on their own again.

Chapter 40

Things settled back into the rhythm of survival.

If you could call it that.

The days blurred together beneath the suffocating heat, one bleeding into the next like sweat rolling down their spines. The sun scorched the gravel road outside, painting waves of heat that shimmered and disappeared before their eyes. Inside, the air was heavy—thick with unspoken dread. No one talked about the night Steve shattered the world. No one dared.

But dread doesn't stay quiet forever.

It started with the knock.

Two plain sedans pulled up at the end of the long driveway, their tires crunching slow, deliberate. Doors creaked open. Out stepped two women dressed in neatly pressed slacks, their clipboards clutched like shields, faces calm and practiced. Strangers, but the kind you knew were dangerous in a different way.

Child Protective Services.

From the porch, Sarah froze, her hands slick with sweat. Mark met her gaze across the yard, his eyes wide. He knew. They both knew.

Inside, Steve stiffened. His posture coiled tight like a spring about to snap. No shouting. No slamming fists—yet. Just a slow, measured stare that pinned them all in place.

Say anything, and you'll regret it.

The words never left his mouth. They didn't have to.

One by one, they were called aside.

First Mark. Then Sarah.

"Do they feed you?"

"Yes."

"Do you feel safe here?"

"Yes."

"Do they treat you well?"

"They love us."

"Do you have everything you need?"

"Oh yes. So many nice things."

Every word polished.

Every sentence rehearsed.

Every syllable a lie.

The social workers smiled. Nodded. Scribbled notes. Their hands soft and practiced, their smiles tight at the corners. Then they left.

The dust hadn't even settled behind their tires before Steve's rage cracked wide open.

He grabbed the phone, beer sloshing from the half-empty can in his other hand, foam dripping onto the floor. His voice bellowed through the walls as he screamed into the receiver.

"You think you're gonna take them from me?"

"Snitch bitch."

"You tell your little brats if I ever see you again—"

He didn't finish.

He didn't have to.

Vanessa unplugged the phone.

She never called back.

He never knew, nor would he have believed that Vanessa wasn't responsible for the visit from CPS.

But Steve didn't simmer down this time.
He didn't fade into his usual cycle of rage and regret.
He got meaner.
Sharper.
Paranoid.
And he made sure they paid for it.

By sunrise, Sarah and Mark were already out in the garden.
Breakfast had been nothing more than water and dry toast-just enough to keep them moving as the blistering sun climbed higher, pressing down on their backs like punishment.

The garden sprawled across the hill, an acre of tangled rows-tomatoes, beans, cucumbers, squash. Hours of stooping and pulling, their fingers blistered raw, their skin red and cracked. No gloves. No breaks.

"Get it done or don't eat," Steve barked perched in the seat of his tractor, a cigarette dangling from his lips like an accusation. Then he drove away, disappearing back down the hill into the house, where the air conditioning hummed and the floors stayed cool.

Mark and Sarah took quick breaks when they could, retreating to the narrow strip of shade at the top of the dirt road. They passed a quart jar between them, sipping warm water that tasted like metal and dust, then returned to the rows of plants, the sun bearing down without mercy.

Mark's real punishment was the dogs.
The pack had grown to twenty pit bulls lined up behind the shed, each chained to the ground with logging chains as thick as his wrist.

They weren't just dogs. They were weapons-in-training. Steve's next side hustle.

But they knew Mark.

When he came near, their tails thumped the dirt, eyes bright with recognition. He fed them, watered them, talked to them softly—training them not to fear, not to lash out.

Steve saw it differently.

"You're too soft on 'em," he sneered one day, beer in hand, watching Mark haul another five-gallon bucket through the dirt. "Gotta make 'em tough."

Mark said nothing.

Because saying something only made it worse.

Sarah handled the rabbits, the chickens, the eggs. She preferred the animals. At least they didn't raise their voices.

But once the chores were done, there was housework.

Not just tidying. Not just sweeping.

Steve decided it was time she "learn how to be a woman."

Canning vegetables.

Folding shirts.

Scrubbing the rust-stained sink.

Freezing okra.

Ironing Steve's clothes with trembling hands.

"You're gonna thank me one day, you're gonna make somebody a good wife," he'd grunt from the porch, smoke swirling like a halo of poison around his head.

Saturdays were for mowing.

Two hilly acres with a rusted lawn mower that wheezed and sputtered like it wanted to die. Back and forth. Back and forth. Hours under the punishing sun, the smell of hot grass and gasoline clinging to their skin long after the work was done.

Sometimes they cried. Quiet tears wiped away quickly.

Crying never helped.

It only made things worse.

At night, the house went still.

But the fear never left.

It soaked into their bones, clung to their skin, filled their lungs.

Sarah counted the days by the buckets of water Mark hauled and the number of times she had to re-clean the same dusty corner.

And every night, they went to bed with aching limbs, blistered hands, and the crushing weight of knowing tomorrow would be exactly the same.

Only worse.

Chapter 41

Steve had a way of making Sarah, now twelve, feel dirty without even touching her. It wasn't just that he was always there—lurking in the background with his half-empty beer and glazed-over eyes—but it was the things he said.

"Look at you, built like a brick shithouse." he'd slur, belching after another swig. His eyes would rake over her, lingering too long, heavy with something that made her skin crawl. "Soon as you fill out a bit more," he'd grin, "you're gonna be somethin' else. Hell, I might just have to marry you myself."

He'd been saying things like that for years.

Sometimes he said it with a smirk, loud enough for his buddies to hear, their laughter sharp and mean. Sometimes he said it alone—his voice low and slurred, his eyes glazed but focused in a way that made her stomach twist.

And sometimes, he said it in front of Hattie.

And what did she do? Nothing.

Just that tired, half-hearted smile, eyes fixed on her beer, her body slumped at the kitchen table while country music crackled faintly from the radio.

Sarah would watch her, hoping—begging—for her to say something. Anything. But Hattie never did. She had checked out a long time ago.

The only person who ever *really* tried to stand up for Sarah was Vanessa, but then, Steve never said things like that around Randy.

But Vanessa had barely come around since John's funeral.

Being in that house—seeing their mother slip further away—it had hollowed her out.

Still, she checked in sometimes.

Quick calls, awkward questions, short visits, careful words.

After CPS showed up, Steve made sure she knew she wasn't welcome.

"She's a troublemaker," he sneered. "Always stickin' her nose where it don't belong."

But Vanessa never stopped asking questions.

When she heard about the things Steve was saying—the twisted slurs about marrying Sarah, about how "pretty" she was gonna be—something inside her snapped.

She waited until she knew Steve wasn't home and called the house.

Hattie answered, her voice flat as stale beer.

"What now?" Hattie sighed before Vanessa even spoke.

"You know *damn well* what," Vanessa fired back, the heat already rising in her chest. "I need to talk to you about Steve."

Silence.

"Mom," Vanessa pressed. "He's saying disgusting things to Sarah. About *marrying* her someday. Do you hear yourself? You think I'm gonna let that slide?"

Hattie sighed again, long and hollow.

"He's not serious. He's just jokin'."

Vanessa's breath caught, disbelief flaring hot behind her eyes.

"She's a *child!*" Her voice cracked, the words trembling with rage. She's not even a teenager yet and he's saying those things about her, *to her* and you think that's a joke?"

The silence that followed was thick, suffocating.

Hattie didn't argue.

"You *have* to protect her," Vanessa said, voice lower now but sharp as glass. "You can't just sit there and let this happen."

"I *am* protecting her," Hattie muttered, her voice soft, defensive. "He's not bothering her."

"*Yet*," Vanessa snapped. "You really wanna wait until he does?"

There was a beat—a long, heavy pause—and when Hattie finally spoke, her words were weaker, like they barely belonged to her.

"I know Steve. He's not gonna hurt her."

"No," Vanessa growled, her voice tightening like a noose. "You don't know him at all."

Another silence.

Longer.

Heavier.

"You keep saying you love your kids," Vanessa whispered, the fight bleeding into grief. "Prove it."

And then she hung up.

She didn't call again for a long time.

And Sarah?

She kept her head down.

She pretended not to hear the words, the laughter, the way Steve's eyes followed her like a shadow she couldn't shake.

But deep down, she knew the truth.

There was a line Hattie wouldn't cross.

Not for her.

And that fall—the fall that changed everything—was just waiting on the horizon.

Chapter 42

The light faded earlier now.

Summer had slipped away, taking with it the long golden evenings, leaving only a sky that turned the color of bruises by late afternoon. The air smelled of dying leaves and damp earth. By dinnertime, darkness pressed against the windows like something alive, rattling the panes when the wind blew too hard.

Inside, the house held its breath.

Dinner had ended, but no one moved. The television muttered low in the background, a grainy blur of static voices that didn't quite cover the silence curling through the house. The wood-paneled walls seemed to lean inward, like even they were waiting for something.

Sarah sat in her chair, tracing the rim of her plate with the tip of her finger.

Steve leaned back, his chair creaking under his weight, a half-empty beer bottle swinging lazily from his thick fingers. His eyes, always half-lidded from drink but never quite dull, flicked toward her like a snake tasting the air.

"Sarah," he drawled, his voice soft. Too soft. "My back's been killin' me again. Come rub it."

Her chest tightened.

It wasn't the first time he'd asked. She'd done it before, stiff fingers pressing into the curve of his spine while he grunted with satisfaction.

On the porch. In the living room. She had learned to keep her face blank, to hold her breath, to pretend she wasn't there.

But this time felt different.

Steve shifted, pushing himself upright with a grunt. His eyes pinned her like a nail to the floor.

"Back in the room," he said, nodding toward the hallway.

Sarah's breath stilled in her throat. She glanced sideways—toward Hattie, who sat at the table, cigarette dangling from her fingers, smoke curling up toward the flickering yellow kitchen light.

Their eyes met. For a heartbeat, Sarah pleaded silently. But Hattie only raised her eyebrows, eyes widening slightly, slowly dragged from her cigarette and turned her head, exhaling smoke like it was an answer.

Steve was already halfway down the hall, the soft *click* of the bedroom door closing behind him.

The sound rang like a bell. A summons.

Sarah's body moved before her mind caught up, her legs wooden beneath her as she followed.

The hallway seemed to stretch longer than usual, the dim light casting shadows that reached like fingers toward her.

Inside, the bedroom stank of old sweat and burn of the hash Steve had recently cooked. The bed sagged under the weight of his frame. His boots lay discarded in the corner, belt draped across the dresser like a coiled snake.

He wasn't lying on his stomach this time.

He lay on his back, hands folded behind his head, eyes fixed on the ceiling.

"Don't be weird," he muttered when she hesitated at the doorway. "You've done this before."

Sarah stepped closer, her heart thundering in her chest, every nerve screaming to run. She perched at the edge of the bed, her fingers trembling as she reached for his shoulder.

"Lower," he grunted, eyes never leaving her face.

When she hesitated—just a flicker too long—he grabbed her wrist. His grip was iron.

He dragged her hand downward. Slowly. Deliberately.

Her breath hitched.

Her body recoiled, but he held her there.

"Stop actin' like I'm hurtin' you," Steve hissed, his voice low and hot against her ear, the stink of beer and sour breath making her gag. "You need to know about a man."

Tears burned her eyes, sliding silently down her cheeks as she froze beneath his hand, her body rigid as stone.

Steve growled when she wouldn't stop crying, releasing her with a shove.

"Jesus Christ," he spat, zipping his jeans. "You're so damn dramatic."

He waved her off like she was nothing.

"Get out," he snapped.

Sarah stumbled toward the door, her legs numb beneath her. The hallway blurred, her vision swimming, the house spinning like it was caught in a storm.

She made it to the kitchen, where Hattie still sat, half-drunk and hollow-eyed.

Her mother turned. Saw her face. Saw the tears streaking her cheeks, the way she shook.

"What happened?" Hattie rasped, straightening in her chair.

Sarah couldn't answer. Her lips quivered, but no sound came.

Hattie rose, reached out—but Sarah flinched away.

"Tell me what happened," Hattie whispered, her own hands trembling now.

It took everything Sarah had to force the words out, no louder than a breath.

Her mother's face changed in an instant.

The dullness cracked.

For the first time in forever, something sharp and bright burned behind Hattie's eyes.

Without another word, she turned and stormed down the hallway. The bedroom door slammed behind her.

Yelling erupted—muffled, angry, sharp.

Then silence.

Sarah sat at the kitchen table, clutching the edges of her chair like they were the only things tethering her to the world. Her body trembled. The light overhead buzzed like a wasp trapped in a jar.

She waited.

Steve emerged first.

He strolled into the kitchen, calm, smiling like nothing had happened. Like it was all a game.

"You did good," he said, the smirk curling his lips. "I'm proud of you for tellin' your mom. That's allI doin', I was tryin' to teach you. So you'd know what's not okay."

Sarah didn't move.

Didn't speak.

Just stared down at the floor, because deep down, she knew.

There was no lesson.

No line that wouldn't be crossed.

And even now, after everything, no one had stopped him.

Chapter 43

Steve had been gone more often lately.

And in any other world, that might've felt like a gift.

But in this one, his absence didn't bring peace. It brought something worse.

Dread.

It slithered through the house like smoke, creeping into the corners, thickening the air until Sarah could feel it in her lungs. Even when Steve wasn't there, his shadow was. Pressing down. Watching. Waiting.

He wasn't drinking as much—not because he was softening, but because he was getting busier. Focused. Calculated.

The marijuana crop he'd planted that spring, tucked between rows of corn and hidden past the creek, had taken off like wildfire. Steve was knee-deep in deals now, stringing together connections that stretched far beyond the back roads of Kentucky.

Some were local guys—easy, predictable.

But others… others came from places like Miami. Names that didn't feel like they belonged here. Routes that were whispered about, never spoken in daylight.

Paducah. Bardstown. And Ray.

Ray showed up sometime in early summer.

He was wiry, with a small frame, narrow face, and eyes that never seemed to blink enough. His smile was too wide. His jokes slid out of his mouth like oil—slick and unnatural, leaving a film on your skin long after the laughter faded.

He never came empty-handed.

Twelve-packs for Hattie. Candy bars for the kids. Always grinning. Always talking.

Always watching.

At first, Steve welcomed him—slapped him on the back, cracked beers together on the porch.

But as the heat of summer settled like a lead blanket over the house, something in Steve began to shift.

He became more guarded. More alert.

He started carrying a pistol. Not just when he left the house, but even when he was home—tucked under his waistband, within reach.

And one night, Sarah saw it.

She'd been heading to the kitchen for a glass of water, barefoot and quiet. That's when she heard the front door open, then close gently—too gently.

She peeked around the corner and froze.

Steve stood in the dining room, breathing hard, hauling in three large black garbage bags from the bed of his truck. He moved fast—paranoid fast.

He dumped them on the floor, unzipped them one by one.

Inside: gallon-sized Ziploc bags, packed tight with marijuana. Dozens of them.

Steve crouched low, counting.

Not just the bags—but stacks of money, too. Thick rubber-banded bricks of bills lined up on the dining room table like little towers.

He kept glancing out the window.

Not just watching—*checking*.

Sarah ducked back into the hallway, heart pounding, breath caught in her chest.

He wasn't just selling anymore.

This was bigger. Organized. Dangerous.

And Steve wasn't just nervous.

He was scared.

Which meant they all should be.

Chapter 44

The cold came early that year, sliding down from the hills like a warning.

By late October, frost kissed the windowpanes, tracing icy veins across the glass, and by November, the garden stood stripped bare beneath a brittle crust of ice. The rows of corn, the vines of tomatoes— all gone. Buried beneath the season's weight.

Summer felt like a lie.

The bonfires, the beer, the roaring voices that filled the fields and echoed through the barn—they disappeared with the sun, leaving behind only the hollow groan of winter winds pressing against the walls.

Steve didn't host many parties in the winter. Not because he didn't want to, but because nobody liked driving those twisting, narrow roads when it turned to slush and black ice. The fields grew still. The barn stayed dark. The nights dragged long and quiet, broken only by the tick of the wood stove expanding in the cold or the wind slipping like a blade through the cracks in the walls.

But the real storm that winter wasn't outside.

It was inside the house.

And it revolved around Mark.

The main job that season was firewood.

Endless firewood.

The stove had to be fed constantly, or the cold crept in, biting at their fingers, stiffening their bones. Steve was obsessed with it. If the fire died down, there was hell to pay.

Sarah and Mark hauled logs from the shed every morning. Stacked them in tight rows on the front porch and beside the stove. Their hands raw and splintered, their cheeks red from the biting wind that sliced through the air.

Sometimes, Sarah woke to the crackle of flames and felt relief.

Other times, it was Steve's voice that woke her—barking from the kitchen, furious that the house had grown too cold overnight. His footsteps falling heavy down the hallway, the clang of the stove door flung open.

But even when the fire blazed, there was no warmth.

Not really.

Because the cold that winter wasn't in the walls.

It was in Steve.

He didn't need whiskey to be cruel anymore.

The silence sharpened him just fine.

And that season, his rage took a new shape—a quieter, more deliberate form.

Mark's report card.

Steve sat at the kitchen table one afternoon, holding the creased paper between his fingers like it was a weapon.

"Stupid little shit," he growled, shaking the page. "You think this is acceptable?"

Mark stood stiff across the room, his gaze locked on the floor.

"You're in tenth grade," Steve snarled, voice rising. "Tenth. And you bring me *this*?" He jabbed a dirty finger at the circled red 'D' on the page. "Explain this."

Mark said nothing.

The silence stretched.

"Get in the corner."

There it was.

The punishment he knew best.

Mark turned, walked to the coldest spot in the house—near the front door, where the draft whistled through the frame. He stood with his nose an inch from the wood-paneled wall, arms straight at his sides, as a soldier standing for inspection.

"Don't move," Steve barked.

Hours passed.

The stove's warmth never reached that corner. The cold seeped into Mark's bones as he stood there, his legs trembling, his back aching. But he didn't move.

Because any shift, any twitch, any attempt to scratch his nose or stretch his limbs—meant worse.

Sarah stood in the hallway, her hands balled into fists. She wanted to scream. She wanted to rip Mark away from that wall. But she didn't.

She couldn't.

Silence kept her safe.

When night fell, Mark dragged himself to bed without a word. His arms wrapped tight around his chest, red welts blooming along his back where Steve had shoved him hard against the paneling.

Some nights, he skipped dinner.

Sarah started hiding pieces of bread beneath her pillow—wrapping slices in napkins and tucking them into his. She never asked if he found them. Never needed to.

The next morning, they were always gone.

No words were exchanged.

They understood.

By midwinter, the house felt like a tomb.

The only sounds were the crackle of the fire, the drag of Steve's boots across the floor, the soft scratch of Sarah turning the pages of her books—though the words blurred together now. She'd reread the same sentence three times, eyes drifting back toward the corner of the room, half-expecting Mark to be standing there again.

Waiting.

The days were short. The nights stretched like black oceans.

Sometimes Sarah lay awake, staring at the ceiling, her stomach clenched tight every time footsteps passed her door. She kept her breathing even. Pretended to sleep. Never moved.

Other times, she looked up and saw Mark, lying stiff in the top bunk, arms crossed hard over his chest, his face pale in the moonlight.

They weren't living.

They were enduring, surviving.

Waiting for the cold to break.

Waiting for the next storm to rise.

Chapter 45

The winter faded slowly—like a bruise reluctant to heal.

The sharp bite in the air softened, replaced by a damp, bone-deep chill that clung to the mornings and soaked into the soil. The snow retreated inch by inch, leaving behind a yard of mud and half-frozen puddles, the land sluggish in its thaw.

But with the melt came no relief.

Spring wasn't freedom.

Spring was labor.

As soon as the earth softened beneath their feet, Steve was barking orders, rallying Mark and Sarah like soldiers on the front lines. The ten acres surrounding the house, silent and frozen all winter, stirred awake beneath a gray sky—and Steve wasted no time reclaiming it.

The garden came first.

The rows stretched farther than they ever had, carving deep scars into the damp earth. A jagged grid, neatly plotted beneath Steve's heavy bootprints, waiting to be filled. Tomatoes, corn, cucumbers, watermelon, cantaloupe, okra, green beans, squash, zucchini—the names rolled off Steve's tongue like threats.

Mark and Sarah stood at the edge of the tilled dirt, the cold soil beneath their worn shoes, the mud clinging to the soles like chains.

Steve's voice cracked like a whip behind them. "Get to it."

And they did.

Knees sinking into the muck, fingers sore from clawing at the earth. No gloves. No breaks. Just the rhythm of planting and covering, planting and covering, while the wind tangled their hair and the drizzle of cold rain soaked their clothes until they clung to their skin.

If they moved too slow, Steve noticed.

If the rows wavered, he noticed.

If a seed lay too shallow or too deep, he noticed.

And he made sure they never forgot.

Every crooked line was an insult to his control. Every misstep was an excuse for the slap of his words or his hands.

The garden wasn't just food. It was proof—proof that Steve ruled this land.

By sundown, the garden sprawled behind the house like a wound, raw and demanding.

Steve stood with his hands on his hips, surveying his dominion while Mark and Sarah barely had the strength to stand.

But the garden was only the beginning.

Next came mowing season.

Two hilly acres of Kentucky scrubgrass, thick and uneven, waiting to be conquered with a rusted push mower that sputtered and backfired like it resented the work as much as they did.

Sarah took the front yard.

Mark took the back.

Hour after hour, they dragged the weight of that machine across the land, their arms burning, legs streaked green, sweat pooling at the small of their backs. The mower clanged against hidden rocks, bucked on uneven patches. Their hands blistered on the handle, raw from the fight.

The air smelled of cut grass and gasoline, and the sun bore down with a growing fierceness that promised worse to come.

But all of it—the garden, the mowing, the sweat and strain—was nothing compared to what lay deeper in the hills.

Steve's real crop.

The one that kept the bills paid and the fear alive.

Marijuana.

He never planted it on his own land. Not once.

He was too smart for that. Too paranoid.

Instead, Steve prowled the neighboring farms under the cover of night—scouting fence lines, checking soil beneath the trees, searching for just the right patch of earth where no one would think to look.

The fields never belonged to him. The crops did.

Hidden in clearings deep in the woods, nestled behind cattle pastures, tucked between rows of corn that weren't his to tend. He marked his territory in places that didn't bear his name, trusting no one and leaving no trace. The only map was in his head—a twisted web of other people's land that he claimed as his own.

"This year's gonna be big," he'd mutter after a few drinks, tracing invisible lines through the air, already imagining the harvest. His eyes glinted with a hunger that wasn't about money alone. It was power. Control.

And every time a neighbor passed the house— eyes cautious—Steve would watch from the porch, leaning against the wall. Smiling that crooked smile like he knew something they didn't.

Because he did.

For Mark and Sarah, there was nothing to do but survive it.

They worked in silence, their bodies sore, their spirits numbed beneath the weight of another season.

But something in them—something beneath the surface—was

shifting.

Not loud. Not sudden. But steady.

Sarah felt it in the way Mark's jaw tightened when Steve's back was turned.

Mark saw it in the way Sarah's eyes hardened when the mower bucked beneath her hands.

The world around them was changing—greening with life, swelling with promise.

And so were they.

Because even as the earth softened beneath Steve's boots, they knew the roots they were planting—deep and silent—weren't the ones he'd planned.

And when they broke the surface, they wouldn't bend.

Not for him.

Not ever again.

Chapter 46

Summer returned like a fever—thick with heat, heavy with unspoken dread. The air buzzed with the drone of cicadas, sweat clung to every crease of skin, and salted cucumbers from the garden were the only relief. But the worst of it wasn't the heat. It was the company.

Steve's circle of friends crawled back like they did every summer, rough men with sunburned necks and voices like gravel. They moved through the house as if they owned it, filling the rooms with sour smoke and mean laughter. Their jokes were sharp, cutting the air just a little too deep, their eyes always looking for something—or someone—to needle.

But that summer, someone new appeared.

Charlie.

Sarah had never seen him before, and that alone was strange. Steve didn't bring in strangers. His crew was tight, a pack of familiar wolves. But Charlie was different. Bigger. Broader. His arms were thick with wiry hair, his beard rough and tangled like barbed wire. He had a slow way of speaking, drawling out his words with a lazy smirk that never left his face. But it was his eyes that turned Sarah's stomach—small, dark, too sharp. Watching. Always watching.

"Who's that?" Sarah whispered, sitting cross-legged on the floor of the bedroom, pretending to help Mark sort through a pile of baseball cards.

Mark leaned closer, his voice barely above a breath. "Heard Steve say he just got out of prison."

Sarah's blood ran cold. "Prison? For what?"

Mark shook his head, jaw tightening. "I don't know. But it ain't good. Don't tell anybody I heard."

The unease settled into her bones. Prison meant danger. And in this house, danger was already too close.

The next morning, Charlie was still there.

Mark's face tightened as they peered around the corner from the hallway, hidden in the shadows.

"Did he sleep here?" Mark's whisper felt like a crack in the quiet.

There he was. Charlie sat slouched at the dining room table, shirtless, cigarette smoldering between his lips. His legs sprawled wide like he owned the place, one boot kicked up on the chair across from him. The smoke curled upward, mixing with the morning light in lazy spirals. And those eyes—sharp, gleaming like a predator eyeing its next move.

Sarah froze as Charlie turned his head, locking eyes with her. His lips twisted into a grin, slow and greasy, like molasses oozing from the corners of his mouth.

She felt exposed, like she was standing there without skin.

Her feet moved before her mind caught up, carrying her into the kitchen, where she grabbed a chipped bowl and filled it with cereal. She could feel him watching, the weight of his gaze burning between her shoulder blades.

She started to ask Hattie—*Who is he?*—but before the words could come out, Steve's voice cut through the air like a whip.

"Take your bowl to your room."

Sharp. No room for argument.

Sarah nodded, head down, cradling the bowl like a shield. She tugged Mark's sleeve, pulling him along.

As they turned away, Charlie's voice slithered through the smoke. "That for me?"

Thick. Slow. Meant to stick in her skin.

Sarah didn't answer. Didn't turn.

Her pulse hammered in her throat as she kept walking, one foot in front of the other, gripping the bowl so tight her knuckles went white.

Behind her, Charlie's grin lingered, slick and heavy in the air like the stink of sweat and smoke.

And he watched her all the way around the corner.

Chapter 47

The night clung heavy to the house, the thick summer heat suffocating even after the sun dipped below the horizon. The cicadas screamed from the woods, their song pulsing through the cracked windows, a relentless hum that felt like a warning.

It was late—too late—when Steve finally called the kids inside.

"Take your shoes off and get to bed," he barked, his voice edged with that familiar bite that brooked no argument.

Mark and Sarah obeyed, slipping off their dirt-caked shoes at the door. They washed up quickly beneath the sputtering faucet, steam rising from the rusty drain as they scrubbed away the sweat and grime of the day. But no amount of water could rinse away the tension that curled tight beneath their skin.

The house was quieter now, though the low thrum of voices still drifted from the living room—Steve, Charlie, and a few stragglers finishing their beers beneath the lazy swirl of cigarette smoke. The television crackled in the background, its sound reduced to a dull, flickering hum.

Sarah was just beginning to drift, the cool sheets pressed against her sunburned skin, when Steve's voice split the silence.

"Sarah. Get out here and give everybody a hug goodnight."

Her stomach dropped, cold and sharp as a blade.

She slipped from her bed, bare feet touching the floor, and felt the familiar sting of dread lace through her chest. She padded down the hall, the flickering kitchen light casting long shadows on the wood-paneled walls.

Steve sat at the dining table, slouched but smirking, his beer bottle dangling from his fingers like a weapon. His arm stretched wide, expectant.

"Goodnight," he drawled, that crooked grin spreading too far.

Sarah stepped close, the air around him heavy with the stench of sweat, stale smoke, and the sour tang of whiskey. She gave him the briefest of hugs, barely touching him before pulling back. But Steve waved her on, guiding her with a tilt of his chin.

"Go on," he slurred. "Don't leave the others out."

Her pulse quickened as she moved around the room, offering quick, hollow embraces to the others. The men laughed, joked, their eyes too sharp. Too watchful.

And then—Charlie.

He stood slow, rising like a shadow from the corner of the room, his bulk towering over her. His arms wrapped around her, too firm, too long, his rough hand pressing against her back in a way that made her skin crawl. The smirk on his face twisted into something darker as his fingers lingered, tracing too low.

She pulled away fast, breath hitching, forcing herself to keep moving, her heart hammering behind her ribs.

But Charlie's eyes followed her all the way back toward the hall.

That night, the fear followed her into sleep.

She dreamed of the kitchen again—clutching that chipped bowl of cereal, Charlie's voice slithering behind her like a snake.

"That for me?"

The words twisted, echoing, growing louder, heavier.

In the dream, his arms were too long, his hands too big, reaching for her, groping, gripping. His smile stretched wide as he leaned in, his breath hot and sour against her ear.

"Come here, Sarah..."

She couldn't move. Couldn't breathe.

No.

She tried to scream, but the word caught in her throat, thick as honey.

No!

She woke with a gasp—her chest heaving, sweat slick on her skin.

And then she felt it.

A hand.

Not imagined. Not dreamt.

Real.

Fingers creeping up her thigh, rough skin slipping down below the waistband of her underwear.

Her eyes snapped open, heart slamming against her ribs.

Charlie.

Crouched over her in the dark, his bulk casting a shadow over the moonlight streaming through the cracks in the wall. His breath rasped against her cheek. His hand moved higher.

Panic exploded in her chest.

Kick. Hard.

Her foot shot out, connecting with his jaw.

Charlie grunted, stumbling backward, one hand flying to his face. The moonlight caught the glint of his teeth, bared in a snarl.

"Shit," he hissed, voice low and vicious.

Sarah scrambled away, dragging the blanket with her like it could shield her from him. Her breath came in short, ragged gasps. She pressed herself into the corner of the bed, eyes wide, fists clenched in the fabric.

Charlie stood frozen for a moment, the dark swallowing his outline.

And then—the door swung open.

He slipped through it like smoke, silent, vanishing into the hallway.

Sarah sat frozen.

Listening.

Waiting.

The house was still. Too still.

She rose on shaking legs, crept to the door, and locked it—didn't care if Steve exploded at the sight of the bolt turned.

She didn't care.

She just wanted it to hold.

Sliding back into bed, she clutched the blanket beneath her chin, eyes locked on the doorframe, her body trembling as the minutes dragged into hours.

And she prayed—silent, desperate.

Please. Please. Don't let him come back.

Chapter 48

Morning came too soon.

The gray light of dawn crept through the cracks in the paneled walls, thin as breath, casting soft shadows across the small bedroom. Sarah sat on her bed, her knees drawn up to her chest, still clutching the thin blanket like it could shield her from the world. Her mind foggy, confused. Her limbs felt heavy. Numb. Hollow. Like every ounce of strength had been wrung out and left somewhere in the night.

"Hey..."

Mark's voice startled her. He stood in the doorway, toothbrush hanging from the corner of his mouth, hair sticking up in wild tufts.

"What happened last night? I saw you run and shut the door, did you have a nightmare?"

Sarah didn't answer. She couldn't. The words sat trapped in her throat like stones.

Mark lingered, his eyes scanning her face with something close to worry, but he didn't press. He just shrugged and turned back to the bathroom, the faint scrape of the toothbrush echoing through the thin walls.

For a long moment, she sat frozen. Then, with slow, mechanical movements, she forced herself to stand and walked to the bathroom. She splashed cold water on her face. Stared at her reflection. But the girl looking back felt like a stranger—pale, hollow-eyed, something stripped from behind her gaze.

She wiped her face dry and crawled back beneath the covers, curling into herself as if she could disappear into the seams of the mattress.

She didn't want to face anyone.

Especially not *him*.

"Sarah?"

Her heart seized.

Steve's voice cut through the silence like a blade, sharp and sudden.

She flinched, her body tightening beneath the covers. Her voice came out barely a whisper.

"G–Good morning."

"Come with me."

There was no room for argument. There never was. She swung her legs out, her bare feet touching the cold floor, and followed him down the hallway. The walls felt closer today, pressing in as they passed.

The living room was dim, the air heavier than usual—thick with cigarette smoke and tension. Hattie and Kathy stood stiffly in the kitchen, their eyes darting between Sarah and Steve. Mark's voice echoed faintly from down the hall, but he didn't come near.

Steve motioned to the chair.

"Sit down."

Sarah obeyed, lowering herself onto the orange velvet seat. Her hands twisted together in her lap, the skin raw where her nails dug in.

"I need to ask you something," Steve said.

His voice was strange. Soft. Almost gentle. But that didn't make her feel safer.

Her eyes stayed fixed on the floor.

"Did something happen last night? I asked Mark and he said he saw you jump out of bed and shut the door."

Her head shot up. Her breath caught in her throat. She could barely swallow. His eyes pinned her in place, sharp and expectant.

"Don't lie to me," he warned, voice low.

Sarah's throat tightened. She looked down at her hands, twisting the hem of her shirt in her lap. Her voice felt trapped, but she forced it out.

"I... I woke up," she began, her words barely a whisper. "He was there. Charlie."

Steve leaned forward, elbows resting on his knees, watching her closely.

Sarah's fingers dug into the fabric. "He was on the side of my bed." Her voice cracked. "I could feel his hand on my leg... going up..." She swallowed hard, feeling the burn of the memory rise in her throat. "He... he touched me. I felt his hand in my underwear."

Steve's jaw clenched, but he said nothing.

"I kicked him," she added quickly, her voice shaking. "Hard. I kicked him in the face."

She finally looked up, eyes brimming with tears, searching his face for something—anger, rage, disbelief.

But Steve just stared at her, his expression unreadable.

"I—I'm sorry for kicking your friend," she stammered, shrinking back into herself, waiting for the explosion. Waiting for the blame.

But instead, Steve leaned back, rubbed his hand over his face, and let out a shaky breath.

"I'm so sorry, Sarah," he muttered, his voice soft, almost breaking. His eyes glistened, red-rimmed. "I didn't know." He pulled her in for a tight hug.

Her body went rigid, the weight of him suffocating.

He sniffled—loud, theatrical—and when he pulled back, his eyes were rimmed red, tears clinging to the edges like they didn't quite belong.

"I'm sorry," he repeated, patting her head like she was some kind of doll. "He said he was too drunk to drive. I didn't know…"

Sarah's skin crawled beneath his touch. She sat still, frozen, her heart pounding so loud it drowned out everything else.

"Are you okay?" Steve asked, his voice softer now, almost syrupy. "Do you want me to call the police?"

The *police*?

Her whole body recoiled at the thought. She shook her head fast, dizzy from the motion.

Steve stood then, his jaw tightening, the fake softness gone from his face.

"Go get your mom and Kathy," he muttered, turning away.

Sarah obeyed. She moved like a shadow, floating through the kitchen.

And then it began.

From where she stood, Sarah heard it unravel—Hattie's voice sharp, panic spilling out in every word.

"Why would you let him in here, Steve? How could you?"

Steve's voice came back low, defensive. "He was drunk. He needed a place to crash."

"I *can't believe* this…" Kathy's voice trembled, breaking apart at the edges. "Child molestation… Jesus!"

Child molestation.

The words cracked through Sarah like ice, each syllable slicing through her chest.

She stumbled back into the kitchen, her fingers gripping the edge of the counter, her body swaying beneath the weight of those words.

Years later, that moment would still haunt her—the way the room spun, the way her breath caught like a fishhook in her throat.

She'd been lucky.

Too lucky.

Charlie, she learned later, had spent years in prison for exactly that. A convicted pedophile.

And he had been in her bed.

Sarah squeezed her eyes shut, but the darkness behind them held no comfort.

Because some nightmares weren't just dreams.

Some monsters came with names.

Chapter 49

Summer slipped away like a ghost, leaving only brittle reminders behind. By October, the wind carried a sharper bite, and the fields that once stretched green and wild turned to gold and gray. The days grew shorter. The mornings, colder. The world quieted beneath the weight of early autumn, but inside the house, the tension only grew louder.

Sarah was in seventh grade now, Mark in tenth. But neither of them felt like kids anymore. They moved through the hallways of their schools like shadows—heads down, shoulders tight, speaking only when necessary. No one knew their secrets. No one could. Steve's rules were ironclad.

Don't talk about me. Don't talk about this house. Don't talk about what I do.

And they didn't.

But secrets like that? They didn't stay buried. Not forever.

Steve had been spending more time away—vanishing for long stretches to Bardstown, Paducah, sometimes Florida or beyond. Rumors whispered their way back to the house. Names like the *Cornbread Mafia* floated through the air, carried in hushed conversations and drunken boasts.

It wasn't just a name. It was a network—a syndicate of growers and smugglers with roots deep in Kentucky soil and reach far beyond. A backwoods cartel that operated with the precision of soldiers and the brutality of men with nothing to lose.

And Steve was in deeper than ever.

Sarah could feel it in the air. The house smelled different now—sour, thick like something rotting beneath the floorboards. The tension pressed down harder with every passing day. Steve was jumpier, meaner, always watching the tree line, seeing reflections only he could see. Always counting the cash that bulged from his pockets. His paranoia clung to him like sweat.

"Violence is part of the business now," he muttered one night, slamming a beer bottle onto the table. "Loyalty. Silence. That's how you survive."

Sarah didn't respond. She just kept her eyes low, her hands busy with the dishes, pretending not to hear.

But something was coming. She could feel it. Like the pressure before a storm.

It came the Friday before Thanksgiving.

Clouds pressed low against the earth, swirling like smoke-stained silk, dark and heavy with what hadn't fallen yet. A sharp wind swept the dead leaves into spirals along the gravel drive. The air smelled like rain, though none had fallen yet. Just a promise.

Just after two o'clock, Steve stepped onto the porch. A cigarette dangled from the corner of his mouth, the flame from his lighter flickering in the wind. He gave a sharp glance toward the road—paranoid, like always—before climbing into the truck.

The engine roared to life beneath him, the old beast rattling down the driveway.

But a mile out, something shifted.

Coming up the road, a line of vehicles. Not just one or two—but a fleet.

Marked police cruisers, unmarked SUVs, and a black van with government plates.

They thundered past him in the opposite direction, gravel spitting under their tires. Steve's chest tightened around the cigarette still burning between his lips.

They weren't just passing through.

He knew.

His hands clenched the wheel so hard his knuckles turned white. For a moment, he thought about turning back. Maybe to warn them. Maybe to face it head-on. Maybe just to watch it all come crashing down.

But he didn't.

Instead, he pressed harder on the gas. His heart pounded in time with the engine's growl. His palms slicked with sweat as the house shrank in his rearview mirror.

He knew it was too late.

The storm had already arrived.

And he wouldn't be there when it tore the house apart.

Chapter 50

Mark and Sarah stepped off the school bus that afternoon with flushed cheeks and light hearts, the November wind biting at their faces as it tugged at their backpacks. Thanksgiving break was so close they could taste it. The promise of slow mornings, warm food, and maybe—just maybe—a stretch of peace.

Mark kicked at a rock, sending it skittering down the gravel road. "I hope we don't have to do anything," he said, voice lazy, eyes fixed on the horizon. "Just sleep, eat, and stay warm."

Sarah smiled softly, hugging her coat tighter. "Yeah… I want to make peanut butter fudge. Like Nan used to."

The words drifted between them like a fragile hope.

But as they passed the neighbor's pond on the left, something shifted. The world, for just a moment, tilted sideways.

People slowed their cars as they drove by, watching. Not waving. Not smiling. Their eyes were sharp. Something odd on their faces, a warning maybe. Pity.

Sarah's gut twisted. "Why are they looking at us like that?" she whispered, her voice barely holding steady.

Mark didn't answer right away. His lips parted as if he might, but then he clamped them shut. His jaw tightened. His knuckles went white around the straps of his backpack.

When he finally spoke, his voice sounded like it didn't belong to him. "I don't know."

But Sarah could see the color drain from his face.

As they rounded the final bend, the house came into view.

And everything shattered.

The driveway was a sea of flashing red and blue. Police cars blocked the entrance, lined up like sentinels. Unmarked SUVs crouched along beside the house. A black van with government plates sat like a beast among them, its windows dark and impenetrable. The lights spun silently—no sirens, just the cold whirl of warning. Their colors flickered across the siding of the house, painting it in stuttering flashes of dread.

Neighbors drove slowly past the property over and over, their faces stiff with judgment and curiosity. Their whispers drifted on the wind like ash.

Sarah stopped dead in her tracks. Her chest seized. "What's happening?"

Before she could bolt forward, Mark grabbed her arm—hard.

"Wait," he hissed. "We don't know what's going on."

But they did.

Somewhere deep inside, they both knew.

They stood frozen, rooted in place as the nightmare unfolded before their eyes. Sarah's breath came in short, shallow bursts. The weight of the past year—the bruises, the secrets, the quiet terror—crushed down on her like a collapsing roof.

The house didn't look like home anymore. It looked like a crime scene.

And then a tall officer broke from the crowd. His boots crunched the gravel as he approached with heavy, deliberate steps. His face was carved from stone, framed by a sweep of white and silver hair.

"You two," he called, his voice sharp but measured. "Come with me."

There was no kindness in his tone. No comfort.

Just procedure.

Mark and Sarah followed him, their footsteps lagging, heavy with dread. Each step closer, the noise grew louder—radios crackling, officers barking orders, twenty pit bulls barking at the invasion. The hum of chaos swallowed the house.

Inside, everything familiar had been torn apart.

Cushions lay gutted across the floor. Drawers emptied, their contents dumped and scattered like entrails. Cabinets ripped open. Piles of clothes and papers overturned in frantic disarray. Uniformed officers moved through the rooms like a swarm, dismantling their lives with practiced efficiency.

Sarah stood in the center of it, numb. Detached. She barely noticed when a gloved hand tipped over the jar of coins she and Mark had saved. The coins scattered across the floor like tiny, helpless witnesses.

In the back of her mind, she knew what they were looking for.

And she knew they'd find it.

It didn't take long.

"Bagged product in the back bedroom!" a voice shouted. "Gallon-sized ziplocks—multiple!"

Another call from the dining room: "Cash in the freezer! Hidden in a coffee tin!"

And then, from the pantry: "Possible cocaine here!"

Mark gave a hollow laugh, crossing his arms tight across his chest. "That's powdered sugar," he muttered. "We use it when we make doughnuts."

But it wasn't just powdered sugar. And it wasn't just weed.

Weapons laid out on the floor of the living room—rifles, pistols, even John Dawson's old shotgun propped against the couch.

Bundles of cash, bound tight with rubber bands, like stacks of secrets.

A worn ledger filled with names, numbers, weights. Evidence of deals made and debts owed.

And across the creek, officers found the worst of it-dog fighting rings in the barn. Chains embedded in the ground. Scarred dogs. Bloodied blankets. Sticks and antlers covered in blood that had been used to pry the dogs off of each other.

Sarah detached and felt as if she were watching the whole scene unfold on a bad television show. The walls of the house pressed inward, squeezing the air from her chest. The sun had dipped low behind the hills, dragging the shadows long across the floor. They reached for her like fingers.

Then a female officer approached Hattie.

Her voice was gentle, coaxing-the kind you'd use with a child.

"Ma'am, I need you to stand up."

Hattie sat slumped in her chair, facing the sliding glass door, a cigarette drooping from her limp fingers. She blinked slowly, like someone waking from a long, drugged sleep. Her cheeks were sunken, her eyes glassy and vacant.

"Please," the officer said again, more softly this time. "Come with me."

Hattie swayed as she stood, her body folding in on itself like damp paper. She didn't speak. Didn't cry. Just moved as if being tugged by invisible strings.

Sarah stared at her mother's back as she shuffled away-small, broken, unrecognizable.

Then came the movement. Quiet, efficient.

One officer knelt beside Sarah and Mark. "Come on, kids," he said gently. "We're going for a little ride."

Mark took Sarah's hand and led her outside, where the blue and red lights still pulsed against the night like a silent alarm. Gravel crunched underfoot as they crossed the yard, the summer heat now replaced by a damp chill that settled in their clothes and made Sarah's skin prickle.

They were guided into the back of one police car-doors shut with a soft, final click behind them-while across the driveway, two officers flanked Hattie.

She didn't resist.

She didn't speak.

Her arms hung limp at her sides as they opened the back door and gently helped her in. Her legs moved stiffly, like her body didn't quite remember how to bend. As she turned slightly, the interior light of the cruiser illuminated her face for just a second-red-streaked mascara, hollow eyes, a smear of ash across her cheek. For a moment, she looked less like their mother and more like a stranger who had wandered into their lives and gotten lost.

Sarah pressed her face to the window, heart aching with something she couldn't name. Not sadness. Not pity. Something colder.

Something like disbelief.

Mark didn't say a word. He stared straight ahead, jaw tight, arms folded across his chest like a shield.

The car door closed on Hattie, and the sound echoed louder than it should have in the quiet night.

She didn't look back.

Didn't glance at the other car.

Didn't reach for them.

She just sat there, head bowed, staring at her lap while the engine idled and the world moved on around her.

The silence that followed was unbearable.

The house-once loud with shouting, laughter, and threats-had gone still.

But the damage was done.

The storm had come.

And nothing would ever be the same again.

Chapter 51

The fluorescent lights in the police station hummed overhead, casting a sterile glow on the scratched metal table and hard plastic chairs. It wasn't warm. It wasn't cold. It just *was*—a holding cell for the forgotten, a place where time didn't seem to move.

Mark and Sarah sat side by side in one of the small interrogation rooms—not suspects, not witnesses, just… loose ends. No one questioned them. Not really. But the way the officers watched them, scribbling notes when they thought the kids weren't paying attention, made it clear they were listening. Waiting.

If they happened to say something useful… well, that would be fine too.

Hours had passed since the bus had dropped them at the end of the gravel road. Hours since they'd stood, frozen in place, watching strangers rip apart their home. Somewhere around 7:00 p.m., they'd been bundled into the back of a police cruiser, neither handcuffed nor comforted, and driven to the station in silence.

No one had offered them food. No one had asked if they were hungry.

It wasn't until a young officer with soft brown eyes and a weariness that clung to his shoulders brought them each a bag of chips and a soda from the vending machine down the hall that either of them had something to hold onto. The chips were stale. The soda too sweet.

But it was something.

Sarah clutched the can in both hands, watching condensation bead on the metal and run down her fingers. Her brain felt hollow, scraped clean by the day's events. She couldn't remember anyone's phone number. Couldn't remember how to ask for help.

But Mark could.

He remembered Vanessa's.

The call went through.

A quiet voice on the other end.

Then more waiting.

Vanessa now had two young boys—Jason, eight, and Aaron, five. She couldn't just drop everything and leave. Calvin had to get them settled, bathed, tucked into bed. The hours slipped by like water through cracked fingers.

The clock crawled toward 9:00 p.m.

And then the door creaked open.

Vanessa stepped inside, brisk and sharp, like a storm dressed in denim. Her hair pulled back, her face tight, carrying the weariness of someone who knew how to survive nights like this. She exchanged a few hushed words with the officer outside the room before her eyes fell on them—Mark, slouched low in his chair, arms crossed over his chest. Sarah, hollow-eyed, fingers still gripping the soda can like it might anchor her to the ground.

They looked smaller than she remembered. Thinner. Their cheeks too sharp. Their shoulders too fragile.

She swallowed the lump in her throat and stepped closer.

But before she could take them home, Vanessa had one more fight to win.

She insisted they be allowed to see Hattie.

The officer wasn't keen. Said it wasn't necessary. Said it might upset the kids. But Vanessa didn't back down. She didn't raise her voice. She just stood there, unmoving, eyes hard as steel.

Finally, they relented.

Down a narrow hallway, past barred windows and heavy doors, they led them to a small visitation room. The air smelled of bleach and despair.

Hattie shuffled in, her wrists cuffed loosely in front of her. Her hair hung limp around her face, and her eyes—once quick and fiery—looked flat, dulled by years of grief and bad choices. She barely reacted when she saw them. No smile. No tears.

Vanessa cut right to it.

"You need to tell them the truth," she said, her voice low but sharp as glass. "You *know* this was all Steve. You *know* it."

Hattie shook her head slowly, her lips tightening like a seam being stitched shut.

"He's not here, Mom. He's not coming for you. He left you to rot. He doesn't care."

Hattie's gaze dropped to her lap, fingers twitching against the cuffs.

Vanessa leaned closer, her voice turning colder. "You're going to protect him? Even now? After everything?"

No answer.

Just silence.

Loyalty to the end.

Vanessa's lips pressed into a hard line. Her eyes didn't soften.

She turned, motioning for the kids to follow.

The ride to Prospect was quiet. The heater hummed, the roads stretched long and dark ahead of them. Vanessa didn't speak. Mark stared out the window, watching the trees blur into shadows. Sarah sat stiff in the passenger seat, her hands resting in her lap, numb.

About halfway home, Vanessa pulled into a McDonald's drive-thru. She ordered without asking. Burgers. Fries. Shakes.

The food came in warm paper bags, filling the car with the scent of salt and grease. The kids tore into it like they hadn't eaten in days, stuffing handfuls of fries into their mouths between gulps of chocolate milkshake. Vanessa watched them in the rearview mirror, her heart breaking a little more with each bite.

They were so thin.

Not just lean—but hollow.

Starved.

The drive from the station to Vanessa's house took forty-five minutes.

By the time they arrived, it was nearly midnight. The street was still, windows dark, porch lights off. The world had gone to sleep without them.

Vanessa led them quietly through the garage and into the kitchen. The soft scent of lemon cleaner drifted through the air, mingling with the warmth of folded laundry piled neatly on the table. Sarah blinked, her eyes adjusting to the soft glow from the stove light, taking in the photos on the walls—smiling faces, birthdays, holidays. A life she couldn't imagine.

"I'll be right back," Vanessa whispered, disappearing down the hall.

Sarah stood in the kitchen like a ghost, not sure what to do with her hands, her body, her heart.

When Vanessa returned, she carried an armful of fresh linens— soft blankets, clean sheets, and a white T-shirt that once belonged to Calvin. She laid them out carefully on the couches, smoothing the covers like it mattered. Like *they* mattered.

Sarah pulled the oversized T-shirt over her head, the fabric hanging loose against her too-thin frame. Mark collapsed onto the other couch, silent. Bone-tired.

Within minutes, they were both asleep—two small bodies wrapped in borrowed warmth, the weight of survival pressing down like a second skin.

For that one night, there were no raised voices.

No threats.

No footsteps in the hall.

Just silence.

And rest.

Chapter 52

Morning crept in soft and slow, slipping through the blinds in faint ribbons of pale light. Sarah stirred on the couch beneath the borrowed blanket, her body still heavy with exhaustion, her mind wrapped in that strange fog where nothing feels quite real.

The house hummed with a rhythm she barely remembered—steady, predictable. The thud of small feet on the hardwood. The rattle of keys. Coats rustling like dry leaves. Jason and Aaron bickered softly as Vanessa smoothed their cowlicks and zipped their jackets.

Calvin stood by the door, lunchbox in hand, boots laced tight. His goodbye was a gentle kiss on Vanessa's cheek and a nod toward Sarah and Mark. No words. Just acknowledgment. The kind that didn't ask questions.

Vanessa caught Sarah's eye as she passed through the living room, offering a small, reassuring smile—the kind that said, *You're safe here. At least for now.*

"I'll be right back," she murmured, her voice low, wrapping a scarf around her neck. "Taking the boys to the bus stop."

Sarah nodded, still tucked beneath the blankets like a child too afraid to let go. Mark barely stirred from the opposite couch, his arm flung over his face to block the light.

The door clicked shut behind them, leaving the house briefly still.

When Vanessa returned, the cold rushed in with her—a sharp breath of November air—but she shook it off like she was shaking off the world outside. She moved into the kitchen with the quiet urgency of someone who didn't need to ask what needed doing. The scent of frying eggs soon filled the air, rich and warm, cutting through the sterile quiet of the morning. Butter hissed against the pan, toast popped up golden and crisp, and glasses of orange juice clinked softly onto the table.

Sarah sat up slowly, the blanket pooling in her lap, eyes fixed on the plate Vanessa set in front of her. Real food. Hot. Made with care.

"You two need clothes," Vanessa said, her voice brisk but soft. "You're not going back there. Not now. Maybe not ever."

There was no argument. No protest.

The house—Steve's house—felt like it belonged to someone else now. Like it had been swallowed whole by the flashing lights and the strangers who tore it apart.

That afternoon, the day stretched out in strange waves. Vanessa piled them into her car and drove to the airport, the hum of the road beneath them almost soothing. Sarah leaned against the window, watching the world blur past—softer now, gentler than she remembered. The sky hung low and gray, the clouds heavy with the promise of snow.

At the terminal, Brandy spotted them immediately. She cut through the crowd like she belonged there—her arms wide, smile bright, California sunshine clinging to her skin.

But as she drew closer, that brightness dimmed.

She took one look at Mark's hollow cheeks, Sarah's sunken eyes, and the way their clothes hung loose off their frames, and her face tightened. Her hug pulled them both close, wrapping them in warmth they hadn't felt in in a long time.

"You guys look like you haven't eaten in a week," she muttered, her voice a blend of love and anger, her arms refusing to let go.

On the drive home, they stopped at a department store. It wasn't fancy—just a place with soft lighting, holiday displays, and piped-in Christmas music. But to Sarah, it felt like stepping into another world.

Vanessa didn't rush. She walked them through the aisles, encouraging them to pick out what they needed—jeans without holes, T-shirts without stains, pajamas soft enough to sleep in without shivering. Brandy tossed a hoodie into the cart and insisted on a pair of sneakers for Mark that actually fit.

When Sarah hesitated over a lavender scarf near the register, Brandy threw it in without a word.

It felt like breathing for the first time.

But the last stop of the day stole the air right back.

The county jail stood silent and looming, its gray walls as cold as the wind that whipped across the parking lot. Vanessa parked and led them inside, her face set, determined.

They approached the front desk, Vanessa speaking low, firm.

"We're here to visit Hattie Dawson."

The officer barely glanced up. His voice flat. "She's not here."

"What do you mean she's not here?" Vanessa pressed, her eyes narrowing.

"She made bail," he replied, flipping a page on his clipboard. "This morning."

"Bail?" Vanessa echoed, her voice sharpening. "Who posted it?"

The officer shrugged. "No number. No contact info. She walked out."

Sarah stood frozen, her chest tightening, her stomach twisting into knots. Mark's arms folded across his chest, his jaw clenched tight.

Hattie had vanished, without a word.

Again.

Vanessa's eyes darkened, her lips pressing into a thin line. She turned without another word and led them back to the car.

They drove in silence.

No one spoke.

The sky outside deepened into twilight, and as they crossed back into Prospect, Vanessa swung into the KFC drive-thru. She ordered enough to feed an army—fried chicken, mashed potatoes, biscuits dripping with butter. The warm smell filled the car, offering a comfort none of them could accept just yet.

By the time they reached home, the street was quiet again.

The house smelled like lemon cleaner and safety.

They ate in silence, pulling apart chicken legs and mashing soft biscuits between their fingers. The food filled their bellies, but not the hollow spaces inside them.

Hattie was gone.

The storm wasn't over.

But for that night, they were safe.

Chapter 53

That night, the dining room glowed gold beneath the soft light of a hanging fixture, its glass panels etched with vines that caught and refracted the warmth like stained glass. The air was thick with the scent of fried chicken, buttery biscuits, and mashed potatoes slicked with gravy. It smelled like home. A place where hunger wasn't something to fear.

The table was crowded—Calvin at one end, Brandy at the other, their laughter bridging the quiet spaces in between. Mark and Sarah sat nestled between Vanessa's two boys, Jason and Aaron, as if they belonged there. As if they'd always belonged there.

But beneath the clatter of silverware and soft hum of conversation, something sharper simmered—watchfulness, worry, the kind that stretched between glances and lingered behind smiles.

Brandy's eyes, sharp and knowing, never drifted far from Mark and Sarah. She watched the way their hands hovered before reaching for seconds, the way Sarah's sleeves swallowed her wrists, the sharpness of Mark's elbows beneath his too-thin hoodie.

"Eat some more," Brandy offered, soft but firm, her brow creased.

Sarah obeyed, though her movements were small, cautious—like any moment someone might snap at her, tell her she'd had enough. She still expected Steve's bark from across the table. Expected the sharp slap of a hand knocking her fork away.

But it didn't come.

She took another biscuit, tearing it into small pieces before nibbling at the edges. Mark spooned another heap of mashed potatoes onto his plate, but his eyes stayed down, his back still tense.

When the last scraps were scraped clean and bellies were full in a way they hadn't been for months, Sarah stood without thinking. Her body moved before her mind caught up. She stacked plates, gathered forks and spoons, drifted toward the sink like muscle memory.

Wiping counters. Washing dishes. Scrubbing floors. That was the price of eating.

But Brandy reached out, her hand gentle but firm on Sarah's thin shoulder. She lifted the plates from Sarah's hands, shaking her head.

"Not tonight," she said with a soft smile that felt like sunlight breaking through clouds. "Go upstairs. Play with the boys."

Sarah froze. The words didn't compute at first. Not work? Not now?

Strange, this being excused. Stranger still to be seen.

She hesitated, eyes flicking to Vanessa as if to ask permission. Vanessa nodded once, her smile softer but just as steady.

So Sarah turned, her limbs uncertain, and followed Mark up the stairs.

Jason and Aaron's bedrooms were a world apart. Soft carpet swallowed their steps. The walls were lined with shelves crowded by colorful books and bright bins overflowing with toys. Plastic trucks and stuffed animals lay scattered like a gentle storm had passed through. The air smelled faintly of cinnamon and clean laundry. A box fan hummed in the corner, blending with Jason's quiet giggles from the next room.

It felt surreal. Too soft. Too safe.

Sarah stood awkwardly at first, her hands at her sides. The toys were too young for her. Too young for Mark. But they didn't mind. They settled onto the carpet, their bodies sinking into the plush floor, their limbs finally able to rest.

For a while, they just breathed. Just existed in the calmness.

But downstairs, the tension that never quite left found its voice.

The murmurs of Vanessa and Brandy drifted up through the floorboards—low at first, then sharper, slicing through the quiet like broken glass. Their voices rose and fell in waves. Heated. Angry. Desperate. They didn't need to catch the words. They already knew.

It was about Hattie.

About her silence.

About her disappearance

About her betrayal.

Saturday came. Then Sunday.

No word. No sign. No call.

By Monday morning, the silence had settled into something heavier. A waiting game no one wanted to play. Mark and Sarah stopped asking. They just lingered by the phone like ghosts waiting for the world to remember them.

Then it rang.

The shrill tone sliced through the quiet like a knife. Vanessa answered in the kitchen, her voice sharp, steady.

She turned toward the hallway, the receiver pressed tight to her chest.

"It's Mom."

Mark froze where he stood. Sarah's breath caught in her throat. Their bodies tensed like they'd been struck.

Vanessa's voice dropped as she returned to the call.

"Where are you?" she demanded.

There was a pause. Whatever Hattie said on the other end wasn't enough. Vanessa's lips pressed into a thin, hard line.

"Are you finally done with Steve?" Her voice cracked on the edge of hope and fury.

The line went quiet. Too quiet.

And then Hattie answered, her words slow, slippery.

"I just need a couple more days."

That was it. No apology. No questions about her kids. No plans.

The line clicked dead.

Gone again.

Vanessa stood there for a long moment, the receiver still clutched in her hand, staring at the wall like it had betrayed her.

Sarah turned away, her eyes burning.

It wasn't surprise.

It wasn't shock.

It was just the next betrayal.

And somehow, that made it worse.

Chapter 54

By Wednesday afternoon, Vanessa's house had transformed into something out of a holiday magazine—at least on the surface. The kitchen buzzed with life, warmth radiating from the oven as roasting vegetables hissed and crackled beneath golden heat. Buttered rolls waited on baking sheets, their soft edges swelling in the warmth, and the scent of cornbread drifted down the hallway, curling around corners like a promise too sweet to trust.

Brandy stood at the counter, sleeves pushed to her elbows, working a pot of steaming potatoes with the steady rhythm of someone who needed her hands to stay busy. The masher clinked against the sides of the pot, her motions purposeful, but her eyes drifted—always drifting—toward the hallway. Like she was waiting for something to break.

Vanessa stood nearby, apron streaked with flour and broth, a sharp knife in hand, chopping onions with precision that bordered on violence. Each slice hit the cutting board with a force just shy of a scream.

It should have felt like a holiday.

But the air was tight. Stretched too thin.

Then the phone rang.

The shrill cry of it sliced through the hum of the kitchen, freezing everything mid-motion. The bubbling gravy, the flicker of candlelight, even the soft scrape of Calvin's boots across the tile. He stepped out from the den, brow creased, and lifted the receiver.

His voice darkened, low and wary.

"It's her."

The words pulled the color from Vanessa's face.

"She sounds drunk... and I can hear music. Voices. It sounds like a party."

Brandy's hand stilled on the pot handle. Vanessa wiped her palms across her apron, her fingers trembling just enough to smear the damp flour across the cotton.

She snatched the phone, her jaw clenched so tight it looked like it might crack.

"Really, Mom?!" Her voice came out sharp, brittle, already teetering on the edge of breaking. "We've been watching the news. We *know* he's a fugitive. And you're *with* him?!"

The words echoed through the kitchen like shrapnel.

"Where *are* you?" Vanessa's voice shook with disbelief and fury. "You should be here—with your kids!"

There was a pause, the line filled with static and the muffled thrum of music on the other end. Hattie's voice slurred through, rambling something about needing time, about not knowing what else to do.

But then, unmistakably, Steve's voice cut through the haze—loud, arrogant, mean.

"I want my kids back for Thanksgiving!"

The words boomed through the phone, slamming into Vanessa like a punch. Her knuckles went white around the receiver. Her other hand fisted the apron at her waist, balling the fabric so tight her fingers turned bloodless.

Across the kitchen, Brandy froze. The ladle slipped from her fingers, landing with a wet splatter onto the tile, mashed potatoes pooling like a forgotten afterthought.

Steam rose from the pot. But the warmth in the room—the soft hum of the holiday—drained away, leaving behind only cold.

The scent of sage, butter, and cinnamon couldn't mask the old stink of fear rising from the floorboards.

Neither of them spoke.

They didn't have to.

Steve wasn't gone. And Hattie—no matter how many chances they gave her—hadn't changed.

Upstairs, Sarah sat cross-legged in her favorite corner of the house—a small sunlit den that felt like a secret garden carved out of the world. Lace curtains stirred with the soft breeze from a cracked window, the fabric rippling like the surface of a quiet pond. A patch of pale sunlight warmed the floor, stretching toward her like an invitation.

A book rested in her lap, unopened. Forgotten.

Her fingers traced the edge of the pages, but her mind drifted somewhere far beyond them.

She was dreaming.

Imagining a life she had never known—a life stitched together from glimpses in other people's windows and the soft edges of movies. A life with slow mornings and pancakes on Saturdays. Where laughter echoed in the kitchen. Where cartoons hummed low in the background, their music a lullaby of safety. A life where the air didn't buzz with tension. Where doors weren't slammed like gunshots. Where someone tucked her in at night—and meant it.

Where her mother stayed.

Where sisters weren't just rescuers—but guardians.

In that sun-drenched corner, wrapped in the soft hush of peace, Sarah let the weight slip from her shoulders. Let herself imagine a life where she didn't have to flinch. Where the world didn't lean in too close, too sharp.

And for just a little while—in that sliver of stillness—she believed it might be possible.

But downstairs, the ghosts were calling back.

And they never stayed quiet for long.

Chapter 55

Thanksgiving morning came thick with tension, like the sky before a storm. The house smelled like it should have felt warm—rich with cinnamon, turkey, and butter—but beneath it all, something sour lingered. Vanessa moved through the kitchen in sharp, clipped motions, stirring gravy with the kind of force that made the spoon scrape too loud against the pot. Brandy barely spoke, her eyes dark and distant as she wiped down the counter for the third time.

Calvin kept to the den, sitting stiff-backed in his recliner with the remote in hand, flipping aimlessly through channels. He knew better than to step into the current swirling in that kitchen.

Because the phone had rung again. Steve had been calling.

Not directly—never directly—but through Hattie, who called with Steve's voice rattling in the background like a snake in the grass. He wanted the kids. For Thanksgiving. For appearances. For control.

Vanessa had lived in his shadow long enough to recognize the trap for what it was-Steve showing up unannounced, asserting control through fear disguised as casual presence. It was never just a visit. It was a warning. A reminder that he still had reach. She refused, her voice steady, her eyes unwavering. But Hattie, worn down and desperate, offered a compromise-just a quick stop, she said, just to keep the peace. The words soured in Vanessa's stomach the moment they left Hattie's mouth. She knew better. She felt it in the tightening of her spine, in the heaviness that settled in her chest. It wasn't peace they were keeping-it was power they were surrendering. And agreeing felt like opening the door to a fire they'd only just escaped.

They would meet halfway. At a roadside convenience store.

Neutral ground.

Just Hattie, she promised. No Steve.

But trust had long been burned away in that family.

By midday, the oven was turned off, the pies left unfinished. The mashed potatoes were packed away without being served. Holiday warmth bled out of the house like heat through a cracked window.

Brandy folded jeans into shopping bags with quick, angry hands. Vanessa helped Sarah and Mark gather up the new clothes they'd barely had time to wear—stuffing socks, shirts, and pajamas into plastic sacks like they were packing for exile.

Mark stood by the front door, shoulders slumped, his bag hanging limp at his side. Sarah clutched a sack of toiletries, her stomach twisting with dread. She didn't know exactly what was coming, but she felt it—heavy in her chest like a stone before the drop.

The sky outside was gunmetal gray, thick clouds sagging low over the hills as they climbed into the car. The tires crunched over frozen gravel, the barren trees along the road reaching skyward like blackened fingers clawing at the sky.

The drive was silent. No music. No conversation.

The convenience store sat off the highway—a flickering fluorescent sign casting a sickly green glow over cracked pavement and oil stains. It should have been nothing. It should have felt safe.

But as the car rolled to a stop, Sarah felt her breath catch in her throat.

It wasn't Steve waiting by the car. But it wasn't just Hattie, either.

It was Paula.

She leaned against the hood of a red sedan, arms crossed, cigarette burning between her fingers. Dark hair fell in sharp angles across her face, heavy eyeliner masking any softness that might have once existed there. Her gaze was unreadable—a woman who knew too much and trusted too little.

Mark stiffened beside Sarah. They knew Paula. Not well, but enough.

Paula wasn't just anyone.

She was the girlfriend of Danny Thompson—Steve's friend, his oldest customer, and now the man hiding him from the law. It had been Danny who bailed Hattie out, who put up his house as collateral. Danny, who kept Steve tucked away behind back roads and heavy curtains, slipping him through cracks in the system like smoke through a screen door.

Danny's place wasn't far. A sagging farmhouse on the edge of town, where he ran a water delivery business. No one lived there for long—not Paula, not their daughter Sam, who'd long since grown tired of the chaos.

Paula had her own place now, just down the road, but it wasn't much. Just enough space to keep her distance. Just enough to keep her sane.

Thanksgiving came and went not as a holiday but as a gathering of shadows. Danny's house was loud with men on the porch, the clink of bottles, the scratch of outlaw country spilling from a busted radio. Women came and went, laughter too sharp, eyes too dull. Steve stayed tucked away, sliding through back rooms, his presence a pulse beneath the floorboards.

But his voice—his anger—echoed through the walls.

Sarah and Mark spent most of their days at Paula's, hanging out with Sam. It wasn't warm, not really. But it was quieter. And the three of them carried enough scars to understand each other without words.

The days blurred together—paper plates stacked with greasy food, cigarette butts crushed beneath boots, smoke curling beneath the rafters like a second ceiling.

And Steve?

Steve made plans.

By Sunday night, with the air brittle and the sky threatening snow, the decision had been made. His lawyer had worked out a deal. He would turn himself in Monday morning, escorted by legal counsel to preserve whatever scraps of dignity he thought he had left.

But the damage was already done.

As Paula loaded Hattie and the kids back into her car, Sarah watched the house fade in the rearview mirror—the sagging roofline, the porch sagging beneath the weight of ghosts.

No one spoke.

The world outside was dark and cold, the fields empty beneath the skeletal trees. But inside Sarah, something stirred—something bitter, something hollow.

They were going back.

Back to the house.

Back to the wreckage.

And no one knew what waited there now.

Chapter 56

Danny had been the one to bail Hattie out.

No hesitation. No questions. Just a signature and a promise. He used his own house as collateral, scrawling his name on the line like it meant nothing.

Because to him, it didn't.

He wasn't doing it for Hattie. He was doing it for Steve.

Danny had scooped Steve up the moment he got word about the raid-before the cruisers even finished lining the gravel drive. Like contraband, Steve was swept away in the blur of brake lights and adrenaline, stuffed into the cab of Danny's truck and driven straight to the outskirts of town. Hidden behind closed blinds and rusted-out sheds.

Danny ran a water delivery business out of his sagging farmhouse, the kind of place that always smelled faintly of motor oil and old smoke. He lived alone—mostly because no one could stand to live with him. Not Paula. Not Sam.

Especially not Sam.

She was sharp-tongued and smarter than she let on. Close in age to Mark, she kept her walls high and her distance even higher. Sam had her own place now-a threadbare house down the road, just enough space to breathe but not enough to feel safe. It was where Sarah and Mark ended up spending most of the weekend.

Not because they were welcome. But because it was quieter.

Paula's place wasn't much better. A leaning porch, a cracked kitchen tile, a half-dead houseplant hanging limp in the corner. But there was food in the fridge. A television that stayed on. No shouting through the walls.

And no Steve.

Danny's house was a different story.

What should have been Thanksgiving turned into a three-day bender-men slouched in lawn chairs on the porch, their boots propped against broken railings. Women came and went, their laughter too loud, too sharp, leaving behind clouds of cheap perfume and crushed cigarette filters. Outlaw country spilled from a busted radio that buzzed louder than the music itself.

Steve stayed tucked in the shadows, slipping through the back rooms like a rat beneath the floorboards. He rarely showed his face, but his voice-his rage-traveled. A slammed door here. A barked curse there. It was enough to remind everyone he hadn't gone far.

The kids stayed out of the way. Mark and Sam sat on the porch swing, watching the grown-ups unravel. Sarah stayed near the door, arms wrapped tight around her middle like she could hold herself together if she just didn't move. The smoke, the noise, the smell of whiskey and burned meat-all of it settled in their hair and their skin, impossible to wash out.

No one talked about what came next.

But Steve did.

He had an attorney on retainer, someone slick and overconfident who promised he could "manage the optics." Steve liked that phrase— "manage the optics." He said it more than once, like it tasted good on his tongue. The plan was simple: turn himself in on Monday with his lawyer at his side. Show up like a man, not a fugitive.

Like any of that mattered.

By Sunday night, the sky had turned a steel-gray and the first whispers of snow drifted along the wind. The air crackled with cold, the kind that hinted something was about to break. Paula didn't say much-just loaded the kids and Hattie into the car with the efficiency of someone used to hauling burdens not her own.

The ride back was quiet.

Outside, the fields were black and skeletal beneath the clouds. Inside the car, the heater ticked and hummed, but did little to soften the chill that had crept into Sarah's bones. Mark sat beside her, his backpack between his knees, silent as stone.

Sarah pressed her forehead to the window. Her breath fogged the glass.

They were going back.

Back to the house.

Back to the hollow shell of what used to be their lives.

And no one-not even Steve—knew what waited for them now.

Chapter 57

Monday morning crept in cold and gray, the sky crouched overhead, thick with clouds the color of rotting fruit, ready to split open. Mark and Sarah dressed in silence, pulling on the clothes Vanessa had bought them-clean jeans, soft T-shirts, sweaters that still smelled faintly of detergent and something like safety. But the comfort of those clothes felt foreign now. Like a borrowed life.

The house behind them was still.

No voices.

No Steve.

No Hattie.

They didn't wait for permission. Didn't say goodbye.

The front door clicked shut behind them, muffled against the heavy sky.

The gravel road stretched long before them, winding through the hollow hills. Every step crunched beneath their feet, each stone grinding like teeth. The air smelled sharp with cold dirt and wood smoke from neighboring chimneys.

Near the bus stop, other kids gathered in loose clusters, laughter bubbling beneath their breath, eyes flicking toward Mark and Sarah like they were something diseased. No one waved. No one smiled.

They knew.

The week before, sirens had ripped through the quiet of their neighborhood, painting the sky in red and blue while the house at the end of the road became a spectacle. Cameras had come. Reporters. Headlines.

And now, Mark and Sarah were the punchline.

They stood apart from the others, eyes down, hearts pounding, every breath sharp with shame.

At school, Sarah disappeared into her routine. She clung to science the way a drowning girl clings to a life preserver—steady, predictable, safe. The rules of the universe made sense when nothing else did.

But that morning, when she stepped into the office to drop off a note excusing her absences, Mr. Rowland, her science teacher, looked up from behind his stack of papers. His brow furrowed just slightly.

His voice softened.

"Was that your house... the one on the news?"

Sarah froze. Her lips parted, but the words fell flat.

"No," she lied, too fast, her throat tight.

He didn't press. But his eyes lingered, reading what she couldn't hide.

He nodded slowly and turned back to his papers.

It was never mentioned again.

But Sarah couldn't shake the weight of it.

She avoided him after that—slipping into classrooms early, ducking around corners, keeping her head down. She couldn't bear the thought of pity. Pity felt like exposure.

Mark wasn't as lucky.

The news had painted Steve like a drug kingpin running a backyard operation, rumors swirling about narcotics reaching local schools. Even though there was no evidence, the damage had already been done.

Teachers eyed Mark differently now. Administrators watched him like a ticking bomb. He was called into the office more than once without reason, forced to sit beneath the flickering fluorescent lights while they asked empty questions and search his locker.

And in the hallways, the whispers burned louder than fire.

Junkie's kid.

Dealer's family.

Mark didn't fight back. Not out loud. But the weight of those stares sank into his bones.

While Mark and Sarah tried to survive the day at school, Steve played a different game.

Across town, his lawyer made the call to the courthouse, offering Steve's voluntary surrender like some magnanimous gift. The moment the call ended, the media was tipped off.

By the time Steve and his attorney rolled into the parking lot, news vans had already staked their ground, cameras at the ready, reporters swarming like vultures around a fresh kill.

But Steve grinned.

To him, it wasn't shame.

It was a stage.

He stepped out of the car like a celebrity, squaring his shoulders, flashing that crooked smile. Flashbulbs snapped. Microphones thrust forward. He soaked in every second.

The booking process was over in under an hour.

Paperwork shuffled.

Fingerprints taken.

Bail posted.

And Steve?

Back on the street before the ink dried.

When Mark and Sarah trudged home from the bus stop that afternoon, the sky hung low, the air sharp with the threat of snow. But worse than the cold was the sight waiting for them in the driveway.

Steve's truck.

It sat there like a predator lounging in the sun, its presence louder than any words.

Sarah stopped first, her breath catching in her throat.

"He's back," she whispered.

Mark clenched his jaw, his fists curling tight at his sides.

He felt it too—that familiar pull of rage and dread.

Inside the house, Steve greeted them like a man returning from a long weekend. He puffed out his chest, his grin wider than ever, basking in his own warped sense of victory.

"Didn't even spend a night in jail," he boasted, spreading his arms wide like he deserved applause. "Outsmarted 'em all. Walked in and out. They should thank me that I didn't blow that place up."

His voice was thick with pride, twisting the truth into something sharp and ugly.

His eyes sparkled like he'd won.

Sarah dropped her backpack quietly, and sat down at the table to do homework, her shoulders tight, her fists clenched beneath the surface.

Mark stood frozen in the doorway, his breath burning in his chest. The walls of the house felt too small. The air too thick.

He was a man who left them behind.

A man who let their mother take the fall while he posed for cameras like a conquering hero.

Mark didn't say a word.

He didn't have to.

It was all there-in the tight set of his jaw, the fire in his eyes, the storm just barely held at bay beneath his skin.

And Steve, bloated with pride and blind to the wreckage he'd made of their lives, didn't notice.

Not yet.

Chapter 58

For weeks, the house lay quiet beneath the brittle shell of winter.

Steve kept his demons on a leash—no drinking, no fists slamming tables, no snarled threats filling the air like smoke. It was the longest stretch of calm anyone could remember.

Without alcohol, he seemed almost human.

Sarah noticed it the way a deer notices the woods going still.

It felt like a trap, but part of her wanted to believe it wasn't.

After all, he was the only father figure left-the only man left at all.

Some fragile piece of her, bruised and tender from losing her real father, yearned for this quiet to be real. Yearned for a morning that didn't start with fear. Yearned for someone who might stay.

And on one bitterly cold morning, she let herself believe—just for a moment.

Steve sat in his usual spot on the couch facing the window, coffee in hand, the crackle of daytime TV in the background. The scent of fried eggs and toast floated from the kitchen, mixing with the soft hum of the kerosene heater. Sarah and Mark curled beneath a shared blanket on opposite ends of the other sagging couch, their backs to the window, half-laughing at the ridiculous contestants on *The Price is Right*.

For one flickering moment, it almost felt like a family.

The driveway outside dipped steeply down from the road, the gravel glistening white beneath the pale December sun. From his chair, Steve could see the top of the hill clear as day.

Midway through a game show round, Steve sat up suddenly, the smile sliding off his face like melting ice.

"Fuck!" he barked, slamming his coffee mug onto the side table, dark liquid sloshing over the rim.

Sarah and Mark twisted around, alarm tightening their chests.

Through the dirty glass, three police cruisers crawled down the drive—slow, deliberate, silent but flashing. Red and blue lights washed over the frost-covered yard, painting it in warning.

Sarah's stomach lurched.

Not again.

A firm knock rattled the front door.

Three short raps. Calm. Controlled.

Enough to silence the room.

Steve stiffened in his chair. No one moved.

"I got it," he muttered, rising slowly. His boots scuffed against the warped floor as he walked toward the door, pausing only to glance back at Hattie with a look that flickered between suspicion and disdain.

He opened the door to two officers-clean uniforms, unreadable faces, hands resting near their hips. Not aggressive. Not relaxed. Just ready.

"Mr. Thompson," one of them said, voice level. "We have a warrant to search the property."

Steve stepped aside without a word, jaw tight, chin high.

The officers entered without fanfare, boots thudding softly across the dirty brown carpet. No shouting. No smashing furniture. Just deliberate movement through the house like they owned the air now.

"Just stay on the couch," one officer said to Sarah and Mark, his voice low but firm.

They obeyed, freezing in place. The children didn't speak. Didn't blink.

The search was methodical. Cabinets opened, contents shuffled through. The back bedroom was swept with quiet efficiency. One man peeled back a corner of the hallway carpet, revealing nothing but dust and forgotten pennies.

It wasn't like the last time.

No broken glass.

No flipped furniture.

But it was still a violation.

Sarah watched from the hallway, her arms wrapped tightly around herself, flinching each time a drawer scraped open. Even when done gently, the sound was sharp enough to cut.

Then-

"Clear," one officer called, voice clipped.

It was over.

Steve exhaled loudly, a puff of mock relief escaping his chest. He shifted his weight, and that smug smile slithered back onto his face like a mask sliding into place.

"That all you got?" he sneered, brushing imaginary dust from his jeans, his rounded belly draping over the front of his waist band. "Hell, you missed the silverware."

A few officers exchanged looks but didn't answer. Most gathered near the front door, already preparing to leave.

But one remained.

The sheriff.

He was older than the others-broad-shouldered, hard-eyed, his face weathered like a boot left out in the sun too long. He stepped forward with a measured calm, drawing a folded packet of papers from inside his coat.

"Steve Thompson?" he asked, voice flat and cold as granite.

Steve straightened a little. His grin tightened. "Yeah?"

The sheriff handed him the papers without a word.

Steve ripped the top sheet open and scanned it.

His smile vanished.

The color drained from his face, then came rushing back in a violent flush.

He looked up, eyes burning.

"What the fuck is this?" he snapped, his voice slicing through the room like a whip.

The sheriff didn't flinch.

"That," he said, quiet but lethal, "is a federal notice of property seizure. This house. This land. The entire parcel—it's no longer yours. It belongs to the United States government."

Steve stared at him. The papers shook in his hands.

"You've got no right!" he roared. "This is my fucking land!"

The sheriff stood like stone. "You can stay—for now. While it's processed. But this place is going to auction. And you won't be here when it does."

The words clung in the air like smoke-bitter, choking.

Sarah's stomach twisted as she watched Steve tremble, not with fear, but fury. Pure, boiling rage.

His grip on the documents tightened until the pages crumpled in his fists. His breath came in sharp bursts, nostrils flaring, teeth bared like a wounded animal backed into a corner.

Mark shifted beside her. She felt it too-the tightening of the air, the way the light seemed to change. Like a fuse had been lit.

Steve had lost the only thing that made him feel like a man.

Control.

Chapter 59

Winter still held the land in its grip.

The fields outside were bare and brittle—broken stalks jutting from frozen earth like snapped ribs.

In the days after the house and property were seized, Steve was like a caged animal—pacing, growling, desperate to lash out. But this time, it wasn't just rage simmering under his skin. It was something sharper.

He wanted someone to pay.

He stewed for hours at a time, spiraling deeper into agitation, muttering about betrayal and how "someone had to've talked." Sarah overheard his hushed conversations with Hattie, his voice low and bitter. One name kept rising to the surface—Ray. Each time Steve said it, the anger in his voice grew tighter, more clipped.

"He's always askin' questions," Steve snapped one night. "Tryin' to be too damn friendly."

He drank, but not the sloppy kind. This was the kind that sharpened his edge. The kind that made him pace for hours, muttering under his breath, reliving old phone calls like he could still win the fight if he just replayed it loud enough.

He replayed the last big deal over and over, like a film stuck on a loop. Ray had shown up late that night. Not his usual grin, not his usual beers or candy bars—just quiet, watching, shifting from foot to foot like he had somewhere else to be. And he'd left early. Too early. Before the count was finished. Before the truck was fully unloaded.

Steve couldn't let it go.

Soon he was on the phone—first to locals, then to old contacts. Half the calls ended in slammed doors or slammed fists. The other half just stoked his fury.

Twenty-four hours after the last call, the air cracked.

His footsteps wore a path in the carpet, his breath thick with beer and resentment. The cold outside had long settled in, but inside the house, it simmered—tight and swollen with something no one could name.

After several more sharp, half-shouted phone calls, he went quiet. Too quiet.

Then he turned, sudden and still.

"I'm headin' to Paducah," he said, grabbing two pistols from the bedroom closet—new ones, bought under the table after his others had been confiscated.

His voice was flat.

His eyes were too bright.

No one asked why.

No one dared.

He didn't load the car with anything but rage. There was no product left—not since the feds had wiped him out.

He disappeared into the night in a 1983 white Ford LTD Crown Victoria—an old law enforcement vehicle he'd bought at a surplus auction, thinking it might keep the cops off his tail. The engine growled low as it swallowed the gravel road behind him, headlights slicing through the trees like a blade.

He didn't come home that night.

By midday the next day, the car returned.

Sarah heard it first—that sputtering groan of rubber across the gravel.

That sound that always dragged the fear back with it.

She stepped to the window, heart hammering.

Steve climbed out alone.

His boots were caked in red clay.

His jeans were soaked and streaked with blood—dark and dried and flaking off at the knees and thighs.

His shirt clung to him like it had been drenched and left to bake in the sun—mud, sweat, and something else.

His face was unreadable.

Not angry. Not calm. Just... blank.

One pistol hung from his belt.

The other was gone.

And Steve wasn't limping. He wasn't wounded. Which meant the blood on his jeans wasn't his.

Sarah stayed in the hallway, just out of view, ears tuned to the voices in the kitchen.

She heard the creak of the refrigerator door. A beer opened. Then Hattie's voice—low, suspicious.

"Where's the other gun?"

A long pause.

Steve didn't answer.

Another pause.

"Wasn't in the truck," Hattie said. "And your pants look like hell."

His response was too muffled to catch.

A chair scraped back. A cabinet slammed.

Sarah didn't move.

Didn't breathe.

She didn't need to hear more.

Whatever had happened in Paducah, Steve wasn't talking about it.

But it was written all over his clothes.

Chapter 60

Things were different after the raid and the following Spring.

Not better—just quieter.

The reckless boldness that once roared through the house like wildfire shrank back into shadows. Steve didn't stop dealing, but his empire withered. The marijuana disappeared from the hills. The kitchen table no longer filled with clippings, sticky scissors, and the sharp tang of resin. The barn grew silent. No more dog fights, no more drunken crowds spilling beer and blood across the floorboards. The circus had left—but the danger stayed.

It just changed shape.

Steve's new customers weren't like the old ones. They didn't deal in pounds or bales. They came alone. They came quiet. Pill bottles rattling in their pockets. Syringes tucked in glove compartments.

And through them, Steve found something stronger.

Dilaudid.

A potent opioid, a white pill crushed to powder, liquefied, drawn into a syringe, and slammed straight into the vein. It hit fast. Hard. A high like nothing else. No stumbling. No slurred words. Just a glassy, detached clarity that left him empty-eyed but sharp-tongued.

It became his obsession.

Steve never drank when he was using—not because it made him better—but because the drugs gave him exactly what he wanted.

Control without the staggering. Rage without the brawl. He didn't throw punches on Dilaudid. He threw words. Sharp, biting, calculated words that cut deeper than any fist.

The eggs were too cold.

The house too messy.

The kids too loud.

And it cost him. Dearly.

By 1987, each hit drained fifty dollars from the household—money scraped from Hattie's monthly Social Security check. Twelve hundred dollars meant to keep the lights on, the fridge full, the kids clothed. But with Steve, it barely covered survival.

Every month, the ritual played out the same. The check arrived. Groceries first—a cart lighter than it should have been—then the drive to the West End. Past boarded-up buildings. Past street corners thick with dealers and desperate souls. To a shotgun house with iron bars on the windows, where Steve's supplier waited.

He always came back hollow-eyed. Twitchy. Sweat tracing the hairline of his scalp even in winter. The car smelled like smoke and sour nerves. And the slamming of the front door signaled the shift in the air.

Sarah felt it before she heard it.

She'd watch him—watch the twitch in his jaw, the restless tapping of his fingers against the worn arm of the couch. Dilaudid made him sharp, but not violent. Not like the bottle.

And for that, she was quietly grateful.

But Mark wasn't.

Mark, now a senior, saw the cracks forming. The refrigerator getting emptier. The stacks of unpaid bills swelling on the counter. The way their mother shrank further into herself, head down, voice small, smothered under Steve's thumb.

And Mark, too, grew restless.

"He's burning through everything," Mark muttered one night, seated on the porch steps. "Blowing it all while we starve, while she just…lets him."

Sarah sat beside him, hands tucked under her legs, listening to the soft rustle of dead leaves scraping against the gravel. She didn't disagree. But fear clamped her jaw shut.

Because she knew the cycle.

When the money ran out—and it always ran out—Steve didn't go without. He clawed back to the bottle. Whiskey. The cheap stuff. Enough to drown the craving for a little while. But when the bottle took hold, so did the fists. The shouting turned to slamming doors, turned to threats, turned to bruises.

And now, the violence came laced with something darker. Something bitter.

Resentment.

When Steve couldn't get his fix—when the cold rush of Dilaudid dried up and the whiskey was all that was left—he wasn't just mean.

He was furious.

A trapped animal, snarling at the world.

And there was nowhere for that rage to go but down.

Down the hallway. Down the stairs.

Into the kitchen. Into the children.

So the house stayed quiet.

But not with peace.

With fear.

Chapter 61

It had been Just over a year since Steve decided Mark and Sarah could no longer share a bedroom.

Sarah was growing—her body betraying her in ways she didn't understand, curves softening into view. And that alone made her a target. One afternoon, without warning, Steve announced it was time. Mark stayed in their shared room. Sarah was moved out.

Into the den.

No door. No privacy. Just a twin bed shoved against the far wall, one scratchy blanket that held the thin, lingering scent of perspiration and tobacco, and a sagging pillow that felt like it had absorbed a decade of anger. The room had once been lined with bookshelves and boxes, forgotten clutter from a life before. Now, it held her.

She didn't argue. What was the point?

That night—like so many before—Steve and Hattie disappeared into the dark, swallowed by bars and beers, returning only when the night was spent. And like always, Sarah was expected to be ready, waiting. Dinner hot. No excuses.

She'd learned the routine.

She sat at the kitchen table under the dim bulbs of the hanging light fixture , pencil scratching across her homework, ears tuned to the sound of gravel beyond the window. The air hung thick with dread, even as the clock crept past 9:00. No headlights yet. No doors slamming.

Mark lay stretched across the couch, eyes half-closed, too tired to care.

They had school the next morning and were told they had to be in bed by 10—no exceptions. So finally, Sarah caved. She cooked. Simple, forgettable. She cleaned the plates in silence. They slipped into bed, hoping to be invisible before trouble found them.

But trouble came anyway.

It always did.

Around 11:00 p.m., the tires crunched down the drive. Laughter, slurred and jagged, spilled in through the thin walls. Boots stomped heavy on the porch. The front door groaned open. Steve's voice filled the house.

Sharp. Mean. Dangerous.

Sarah squeezed her eyes shut, feigning sleep, pulling the thin blanket up to her chin, her body stiff with anticipation.

And then it came—the words she dreaded:

"This shit is cold!"

Footsteps thundered toward the den. She felt them before she heard them. The floor trembled beneath her bed.

The silhouette of Steve filled the doorway, his body swaying. In one hand, a pork chop—cold, greasy, forgotten.

In a flash, he smashed it into her face.

The sharp bone caught her nose, slicing across her eye. Grease smeared her cheek. Salt and shame burned her skin. She gasped, her breath catching between a scream and a sob.

"I'm sorry," she stammered, wiping the meat from her face with shaking fingers. "I didn't know when you were coming back—I'm sorry—"

But sorry meant nothing.

Steve grabbed her by the arm, yanking her out of bed, dragging her into the kitchen like a rag doll.

He swept the countertop clean in one violent motion—plates, forks, dish towels—all crashing to the floor. The sound echoed in the hollow house like glass shattering inside her.

"Clean it up!" he barked, voice slurred but razor-sharp.

Sarah dropped to her knees, fingers trembling as she gathered the broken pieces of the night. The dish towel. The fork. The shattered sliver of hope that maybe tonight would've been different.

She scrambled to cook again. Not for herself. Not for Mark.

For him.

Steve slumped on the couch, a king on his throne, waiting for his feast. The television flickered mindlessly. Cigarette smoke curled toward the ceiling. The saltshaker sat beside him like a relic, ready for him to anoint his meal.

Sarah brought him the tray, arranged carefully with the plate to the left napkin and silverware on the right. Her hands shaking so hard the fork clinked against the plate. She kept her eyes low.

He ate slowly, chewing with exaggerated disgust, smacking his lips like a punishment. Then, mid-bite, his head lolled back.

Asleep.

She stayed frozen on the floor near his feet, knees folded beneath her, holding her breath.

When she finally reached for the tray, his eyes snapped open.

"Don't touch my fuckin' food while I'm eatin'!"

The words lashed out, sharp as a blade.

She jerked her hands back, swallowing hard. He finished his last few bites, then flipped the tray onto the floor in front of her with a sneer.

"Clean this shit up. Go to bed."

She obeyed.

But that night, sleep didn't come. Not fully. Not really.

Mark shook her awake at dawn, gentle fingers brushing her shoulder.

"C'mon," he whispered. "We'll be late."

He didn't fully know what had happened. Although he heard the chaos, he could only imagine what was happening. But he saw the swelling at the corner of her eye. The cuts across her nose and eyelid.

Sarah said nothing.

But she had made a decision.

That night, in the dark, she crept to the kitchen. Dug through the drawer until she found it—the little black phone book Hattie always kept tucked beneath old takeout menus. Her fingers flipped through the pages until she found it.

Brandy.

California.

The only way out.

She wouldn't get on the bus that afternoon. She'd find the payphone outside school. She'd call. She'd make a plan.

But Steve knew her too well.

At lunchtime, the intercom crackled:

"Sarah Dawson to the office."

When she and Hattie exited the school, he was waiting, leaning against the frame of the car, a sack of fast food in one hand, a lopsided smile carved across his face.

"C'mon, sweetheart," he said smoothly. "Thought we would take you out for the day."

They drove in silence.

He stopped for ice cream on the way home, handing her the cone like a bribe.

"I'm sorry," he murmured. "That shouldn't've happened. It won't happen again."

The words rattled, empty.

Sarah smiled.

She nodded.

She played along.

Because that's what survival looked like now.

Chapter 62

Summer came with a heavy heat and harder truths.

Mark graduated high school that June—a milestone most kids celebrated with balloons and cake, a ticket to freedom. But freedom wasn't for him. Not yet.

Steve made that clear.

"Get a job or get out."

Mark wanted to leave—wanted it so bad he could taste it. But Sarah was still there. Still trapped under Steve's thumb. He couldn't walk away. Not yet.

So he stayed.

A neighbor down the road worked for a house-moving company— the kind that lifted entire homes off their foundations and hauled them across counties. Brutal work. The kind that cracked your hands and burned your skin, left your muscles screaming. But it paid. And Mark took the job, rising before dawn, coming home coated in sweat and dust, every step weighted by exhaustion.

Steve? He wasn't about to sweat for a living.

Not when Danny Thompson could hand him cash under the table.

Water deliveries. Hauling heavy tanks to farms and rural homes. Enough to keep the Dilaudid flowing, enough to keep up appearances.

Mark worked to keep the house standing. Steve worked to keep himself numb.

And Sarah?

She worked for both of them.

Every summer, the garden returned—an acre-wide plot at the top of the hill behind the house, carved into the ground like rows scars. Rows of corn, tomatoes, okra, squash, watermelon. Steve loved to boast about that garden. About the size, the yield, the *hard work* it took to grow it. But once the seeds were in the ground, his hands stayed clean.

It was Sarah's burden.

Every morning before the sun climbed up in the sky, she slipped on her worn sneakers, grabbed a couple slices of dry toast, and hiked the steep hill with a mason jar of water in hand. The dew clung to her calves. The hoe felt heavy before she even lifted it. Day after day, she tilled, weeded, watered—alone in that field, sweating under the weight of summer.

There was a kind of peace in it.

The quiet of the garden, the early stillness before the heat settled in.

But it was work. Back-breaking, unending work.

She filled baskets and buckets with green beans until her fingers blistered, carried armloads of squash so heavy they left welts on her arms. The tomatoes ripened faster than she could pick them, their skins splitting under the weight of the sun.

After the harvest, the work didn't stop.

The kitchen turned into a furnace—jars clinking, pots boiling, the air thick with the sour tang of tomatoes and vinegar. Sarah stood at the stove for hours, washing jars in water that never stayed clean, wiping sweat from her brow as she listened to the lids pop and seal.

But no matter how much she did, it wasn't enough.

The weeds always crept back in, climbing between the rows like they owned the place. She couldn't fight them all. Not alone. Not with the heat. Not with the hillside turning to dust beneath her feet.

And that's when Steve decided to care again.

One afternoon, he stood at the edge of the garden, arms crossed, jaw clenched, surveying the rows like a king inspecting his ruined kingdom.

"You haven't done shit all summer."

Sarah stood there, her shirt clinging to her skin, her arms streaked with dirt. Her hands were raw, her knees cracked from crouching in the mud. But Steve didn't see that.

Or maybe he did.

And just didn't care.

He needed a reason to stop working for Danny.

The garden became his excuse.

"It's bein' neglected," he spat to anyone who'd listen.

"Gotta stay home. Get things in order."

But the truth was simpler. Steve didn't want to work.

He never blamed himself. He needed someone else to carry that weight. Someone to point to when the world asked why the garden failed, why the bills piled up, why the house rotted beneath its own roof.

And Sarah, always there, always silent, became the scapegoat.

Meanwhile, Evan—ever the golden boy—was now old enough to drive. He visited more often, slipping into the seat beside Steve, windows down, radio blaring, the two of them grinning like they owned the world.

Mark, now with paychecks in his pocket, was allowed into that circle more often. He wasn't "the lazy kid" anymore. He was an asset. A man. Someone Steve could brag about to his buddies, but also a source of cash to fund his habit.

Now Steve had his boys.

And Sarah?

She became the problem.

The burden.

The disappointment.

The garden wasn't just dirt and plants—it was her reflection in Steve's eyes. Every weed, every brown leaf, proof that she was failing. Proof that she wasn't enough.

She wasn't the girl in the kitchen, boiling jars with care.

She was the scapegoat.

The thing Steve couldn't control.

The last piece left to break.

Chapter 63

The cycle continued.

Drugs. Anger. Drinking. Rage.

It had become the rhythm of the house—predictable in its unpredictability. A song played on broken strings, discordant but familiar.

Sarah moved through it like a shadow, learning the notes by heart. She knew the tilt in Steve's voice when he was high, the weighted shuffle of his footsteps when the bottle had taken hold. The subtle shifts. The storm signs.

It was the fall of her junior year.

Her sixteenth birthday.

She came home from school that day carrying the faintest flicker of hope—small, fragile, but there. Not for cake or candles or anything so grand. Just a glance. A word. Some sign that someone remembered.

The house was quiet when she walked in.

Too quiet.

Steve was gone. Mark sat hunched on the edge of the couch, watching football, his face pale, his eyes tired. Evan lounged across the recliner, arms behind his head, doing what Evan did best—nothing.

Rain had fallen steady all day, turning the gravel road into thick rivers of red clay. Mark's job had been canceled. Evan hadn't worked in months. He lived like Steve, shifting his weight from one worn cushion to another, letting the world fall on someone else's shoulders.

The air inside was sour—stale cigarette smoke, damp clothes, old fear.

Sarah slipped quietly into the kitchen, set her books down on the table. She didn't expect a celebration. But a part of her, deep down, still ached for it.

Steve came home about an hour later.

His eyes were glassy, his words slurred—a dangerous mix of too much Dilaudid and whatever whiskey he'd found to wash it down. Hattie trailed behind him, swaying under the weight of her own emptiness, cigarette clutched between two trembling fingers, beer in her other hand.

They came in laughing. Loud. Careless.

Sarah stood by the doorway, waiting for the moment to pass, for the storm to move on.

But Evan spoke.

Too loud.

Too casual.

"Hey, it's her birthday."

Steve's head turned slowly, his eyes focusing on Sarah like she was something new—something he'd just remembered was there.

The smile that spread across his face made her skin crawl.

Without warning, he lunged from the couch, darted across the room, catching her off guard. His hands grabbed her arms—rough, unrelenting—and he threw her backward onto the loveseat she'd once used as a bed..

The breath left her lungs in a gasp. She tried to push up, to scramble away, but he was already on top of her, pressing his full weight down until she couldn't move.

"Sixteen," he slurred, rocking his hips in a grotesque parody of sex. "Old enough to fuck."

His laugh—raw and jagged—ripped through the room.

Sarah froze beneath him. Her heart raced, her throat clamped shut. The world tilted sideways. She couldn't move. Couldn't scream.

Hattie stood at the stove, her back turned, stirring something in a pot that probably wasn't even hot anymore. Smoke curled lazily from her cigarette, rising into the air like surrender. She didn't turn around. She didn't speak, too afraid to intervene.

Sarah's body shook beneath the weight pressing into her chest, but she didn't cry. She couldn't. She felt outside of herself, watching from somewhere far away.

When Steve finally pulled back, he hit her hard across the face—not a slap meant to sting, but a blow meant to remind. Her head snapped sideways, the heat rising instantly beneath her skin. He laughed as she crumpled inward, clutching her cheek, swallowing the cry that threatened to break free.

Then he walked over and dropped back into his dent in the couch, reclaiming it like a throne, as if nothing had happened.

Sarah sat frozen in place.

The couch still held his warmth. She pushed herself up slowly, trembling, her legs unsteady. She made her way back to the dining table, where her books lay open, her homework unfinished.

She sat down.

She tried to read.

She tried to breathe.

But the tears slid down anyway, pooling onto the pages, blurring the ink until the words melted away.

Evan passed behind her, paused for a moment, his hand on the back of her chair.

"I'm sorry," he mouthed.

She didn't look at him.

Didn't care.

It didn't matter.

She was sixteen now.

And wanted to be invisible.

She had dreamed once of escape.

Tried to call Brandy. Tried to run.

Steve had stopped her back then—before the raid, before the house was seized, before everything collapsed in on itself.

He blamed her sisters for that.

"You think you're better than us," he hissed at her one night, his breath hot and bitter. "Just 'cause you don't drink. Just 'cause you sit there like some little princess with your nose in a book."

But she wasn't trying to be better.

She was trying to survive.

School was her last refuge. Science, her sanctuary. She poured herself into college applications, circling distant states on the map— Colorado, Oregon, Montana—anywhere the air was clean, the sky wide, and the silence didn't carry the weight of dread.

Somewhere she could be free.

But for now?

For now, the only thing no one could take from her was the dreaming.

Chapter 64

By the following summer, the illusion finally cracked.

The house—the same one Sarah had scrubbed, weeded, bled for—was no longer theirs. After the raid and seizure, the government held the deed like a sword over their heads, but Steve refused to swing it. Mortgage payments stopped cold. He wasn't about to hand over money for a place he claimed had never truly belonged to him—never mind that it had never been *his* money. That had always been Hattie's check, and now he had better use for that money—his vein.

And when Mark turned eighteen, the Social Security checks shrank from barely manageable to impossible. Eight hundred dollars a month. Barely enough to feed his habit, let alone the family.

It unraveled fast.

But Steve was never one to sit idle when there was a scheme to hatch. Somewhere in a neighboring county, he sniffed out opportunity. An old white farmhouse, worn at the edges but still standing, owned by an elderly couple who'd grown tired of the tenant refusing to leave. They wanted her gone. The place sat rotting under her hoard—decay behind closed doors.

Steve offered them a deal.

"If I can get her out," he said, flashing that snake-oil grin, "you rent it to me. Three-fifty a month."

The old couple agreed. Desperation speaks louder than reason.

Days later, Steve showed up at the woman's doorstep. Sarah never heard the words he used, but she could imagine the tone—the smooth menace, the threat tucked just beneath the surface. Whatever it was, it worked. Within a week, she was gone. Vanished like smoke. But the house she left behind?

It was hell.

The second the door creaked open, the stench hit like a punch to the throat—rotted food, sour diapers, mountains of trash stacked to the ceiling, walls yellowed with filth. A hoarder's kingdom, left to fester.

And that's when Steve drafted his army.

He loaded Hattie, Mark, and Sarah into the truck—Evan, of course, exempt from such duties—and marched them straight to the farmhouse. Armed with trash bags, cracked buckets, and cheap bleach, they spent a week elbow-deep in decay. Hauling liquefied garbage through the sweltering Kentucky heat, peeling old food from the floor with putty knives, scraping walls stained with lives no one wanted to remember.

Only when the last bag hit the landfill did Steve deem the house livable.

From the outside, the farmhouse had a ghost of charm. Faded white paint, a wide front porch with sagging columns, cracked concrete steps worn soft by time. The backyard held a small barn-shaped shed, red paint flaking like dried blood, and a patch of dirt waiting for a garden. The land whispered *possibility*—if you didn't look too close.

Sarah clung to that whisper like it might save her.

"Can I paint the rooms?" she asked one afternoon, her voice barely a breath.

Steve grunted, indifferent. "Long as it don't cost me nothin.'"

And so, she painted.

Negotiated with the landlords—paint deducted from rent. A rare win. She spent that summer in a cocoon of soft blues and muted whites, her roller gliding over cracked plaster, burying the stains and ghosts beneath layers of color. She painted like it mattered. Like she could carve out some corner of peace, some beauty in the ugliness.

It was different from the summers before. No acre of garden to tend. No hours sweating under the sun, weeding rows that never stayed clear. No dogs to tend, they had all been sold or taken behind the barn and shot before the move.

Just walls. What's wrong

Just paint.

Just a hope that maybe, if she covered enough of the past, the present might feel lighter.

But the quiet didn't last.

With the move, Mark lost his job with the house-moving crew. His ride—the neighbor Rick—was no longer close enough to ride with, and with no transportation, the paycheck dried up. And without income, Mark became dead weight in Steve's eyes. A liability. An inconvenience.

So, Steve forced him into the Army.

Didn't ask. Didn't debate.

"You're gonna do somethin' with your life," Steve spat, as if *he* had built anything but ruin. "Get out and make yourself useful."

Mark, who had always been Sarah's anchor, her shield, packed his duffel bag and climbed into the car that would drive him away. She stood on the porch and watched the taillights disappear down the road, her hands limp at her sides.

She didn't cry—not in front of him. Not until the truck was gone.

Because when Mark left, so did her last tether to safety.

The farmhouse walls stood freshly painted. The summer heat hummed outside. But inside, everything felt thinner.

Like something was fraying.

About to snap.

And Sarah knew, as sure as the sun would set—that it was about to get worse.

Much worse.

III

Part Three

Alone in the Fire.

Chapter 65

By late summer, Steve's days settled into a splintered, toxic rhythm.

Most mornings, he vanished into the West End, chasing that sharp burn of Dilaudid, slipping behind sagging doors and smoke-thick rooms that reeked of something sordid. Other days, when the needle didn't call, it was wine and whiskey down by the river bottoms—cheap and endless, shared with the rough crowd from a few doors down. Men who didn't ask questions. Men who didn't care.

On drug days, Steve paced like a caged animal—snapping, whining, muttering curses at shadows no one else could see.

On drinking days, he was worse. Dangerous.

The farmhouse creaked beneath it all.

There were two bedrooms upstairs, but Sarah wasn't allowed to use them. With Mark gone and Evan drifting in and out like smoke—there when it suited him, gone when it didn't—the upstairs stayed hollow, gathering dust. Sarah's space was a narrow stretch between the kitchen and living room, not much more than a wide hallway pretending to be a room.

Her bed sat low to the ground beside a single window, its pane streaked with grime. A tattered curtain, strung across with fraying yarn, offered the illusion of privacy. But it didn't stop the sounds.

Nothing ever stopped the sounds.

From her corner, she heard everything—Steve's boots scraping against the wood floor, the clink of his whiskey bottle against the table, the gravel scrape of his laugh when the liquor bit too hard. His and Hattie's bedroom sat just beyond the living room, past the sagging recliner and the worn couch, both of them too drunk most nights to bother closing the door.

And the only bathroom in the house?

Off the kitchen.

Right past Sarah.

Every flush, every footstep, every creak of the floorboards crossed her like an invisible hand.

But it was the footsteps at night that she hated most.

One night, she jolted awake, heart racing, the weight of her own breath suffocating. For a moment, she thought she was back in the old house. Thought Charlie's shadow loomed beside her bed again.

But it wasn't Charlie.

It was Steve.

At first, she told herself it was an accident—he'd stumbled half-drunk on his way to the bathroom, lost his footing in the dark. He'd crouched near her bed without realizing.

But then it happened again.

And again.

He sat on the side of her bed in the dark, the sour stench of body odor and whiskey thick on his breath. His hand slid beneath the thin blanket, fumbling, rough, wandering where it had no right to be-groping her chest, pressing against her stomach, fingers tugging at the hem of her shirt.

At first, she harshly whispered, "Stop!"

Tried to roll away.

But the more she resisted, the meaner he got. His breath hissed against her ear, threats slurred and sharp, reminding her what would happen if she ever told. Reminding her who held the power.

There was no one to tell anyway.

Hattie slept on, mouth open, beer resting in her slack hand, the television flickering across her vacant face. She wouldn't wake. And if she did—she wouldn't stop him. She never had.

So Sarah stopped resisting.

Each night bled into the next—his rough hands, his muttered apologies that came too late, the way he patted her shoulder afterward like it made things right. She lay stiff as stone beneath the blanket, eyes closed, drifting far away.

Mountains.

Oceans.

Anywhere but here.

Tears soaked into her pillow, silent and endless.

And every morning, she rose like nothing had happened.

Because that was how you survived.

Chapter 66

The weight of the move didn't truly settle on Sarah's shoulders until the first day of school—her senior year.

That was when it hit her—not all at once, but slow and bruising—like a dull ache that sank behind her eyes and stayed there. She wouldn't be graduating with the kids she'd known since the fourth grade. No familiar faces in the halls. No easy rhythm of belonging. Just strangers.

The hallways of this new school felt too bright, the chatter too sharp, the lockers lined up like soldiers dressed in colors she didn't recognize. Everything smelled like lemon-scented floor cleaner and someone else's perfume. A world that wasn't hers.

She told herself it didn't matter.

Keep your head down. Get through the year.

But by this point, friendship came with expectations—weekend outings, football games, late-night drives in rusty hand-me-down cars. Girls her age had their own set of keys, their own circles, their own freedoms.

Sarah had none of it.

She didn't even have the words to explain why.

Better not to make friends at all, she reasoned, than to make excuses. Better to stay invisible than let anyone close enough to see the cracks.

Still, despite her best efforts, a few kind faces pushed through—kids who smiled in the hallways, who noticed when teachers turned their backs, who offered her a seat without asking for anything in return. Among them was Michelle.

A senior like Sarah. Soft-spoken, but not shy. Confident in the way some girls could be—without being cruel about it. They shared a class and, over time, their conversations turned from homework to something lighter. Easier.

One afternoon, Michelle leaned across their desks, her hair falling into her eyes.

"Hey, you wanna come over Friday night? Watch some movies? My parents'll be out to dinner."

Sarah hesitated.

No one ever invited her anywhere.

She smiled, half out of habit, half out of disbelief.

"I could even pick you up," Michelle added, sensing the reluctance. "Bring you home after."

It sounded so simple. So normal. Sarah wanted to say yes. God, she wanted to say yes.

But permission? Asking Steve? That was a minefield.

Still, that night, her heart pounding like she'd done something wrong already, Sarah approached him. He sat slouched in the recliner, a beer in one hand, the TV flickering shadows across his face.

"I got invited to a friend's house," she said carefully. "Just for movies."

Steve narrowed his eyes, taking a slow sip.

"Who?" His voice low. Suspicious.

"Michelle. She's in my class."

He studied her, leaned back, and smirked.

"No boys?"

Sarah shook her head fast. "Just her."

He stared a little longer. Then, shockingly, he nodded.

"I want to meet her."

Sarah blinked. "Okay…"

"Make sure you're not lyin'."

Friday came like a slow-brewing storm. Sarah spent the whole day with her stomach twisted in knots.

Michelle pulled into the driveway right on time, her small blue Ford Ranger humming softly beneath the weight of the moment. Sarah hovered near the window, watching as Michelle stepped out, smiling, confident in the way people with good lives could be.

Steve answered the door.

Sarah couldn't hear what was said—only saw the way he leaned in the doorway, eyes sweeping over Michelle like he was inspecting a piece of furniture. Slow. Calculating. Michelle smiled through it, polite, unaware.

Finally, he waved Sarah out.

She walked to the car like someone crossing a frozen lake—half expecting it to crack beneath her feet.

But in Michelle's house, the world softened.

They watched movies, ate popcorn, laughed about nothing. Sarah sat on the couch and felt… normal. For a little while, she wasn't the girl with secrets. She wasn't trapped.

Then, near midnight, the front door creaked open.

Michelle smiled, standing up. "That's my brother, Brad."

Sarah glanced up, startled.

Brad was taller, sandy-haired, maybe a couple of years older. He nodded politely, offered a quiet hello, then disappeared into the kitchen.

Sarah barely thought twice about him.

But the next morning, back at home, the phone rang.

Steve answered.

Sarah heard it—the way his tone shifted. Curious. Amused.

He turned toward her, grinning.

"It's for you. Some guy named Brad."

The floor dropped beneath her.

Michelle must've given her brother the number.

Brad wanted to ask her out.

Sarah took the phone with shaking hands. Her voice was light, polite, playing the part. She politely declined. Thanked him for calling.

But when she hung up, Steve's face had changed.

The grin was gone.

His jaw tightened. His eyes darkened.

And Sarah could feel the temperature shift—the calm before the storm that was already rolling in.

She stood there, phone still warm in her hand, knowing that door she'd cracked open?

It should've stayed shut.

Chapter 67

It didn't take long for everything to unravel.

Steve had let her leave with Michelle. He'd even allowed her to answer the phone when Brad called. But none of that meant trust. It meant a test—a trap set with the cruel patience of a spider.

By nightfall, the liquor had dug its claws into him again, and the accusations began.

"You used that girl as a cover," he slurred, leaning heavily in the doorway, eyes bloodshot, voice thick with venom. "You went over there to fuck that boy. Don't lie to me."

Sarah sat frozen on the couch, her hands knotted tightly in her lap, eyes locked on a crack in the chipped tile beneath her feet.

She didn't answer.

There was no point.

The silence only fanned the flames.

Steve prowled the living room, knocking an ashtray across the room, cursing low under his breath, before he spun suddenly, landing back on her like a hammer.

"You remember what happened with Charlie?" His voice sliced through the quiet.

Sarah's heart seized.

"I asked you a question. Tell me again. Tell me *exactly* what happened."

Her stomach twisted. She knew better than to refuse.

So she told him.

Again.

She told him about the night Charlie crouched beside her bed, his hand sliding beneath her clothes, the sick heat of his breath against her skin. She recited it flatly, like reading from a police report. The same words she'd spoken before, back when she was just a child, trembling as Steve pretended to care.

But this time, there was no pretense.

He exploded.

"You fucking *whore,*" he spat, the word crashing into her like a slap. "You never told me *that* part. If I'd known that, I would've handled it different."

Sarah flinched, her breath shallow.

"I *did* tell you," she whispered.

"No, you didn't. And, you didn't—because you *liked* it. That's why you didn't say nothing."

The word *whore* spilled from his lips again, over and over, loud enough to echo off the walls. He wasn't speaking to her anymore. He was branding her, writing it into her skin.

Sarah pressed her lips together, refusing to cry. Not this time. She knew the truth, she'd never even held hands with a boy.

Steve stormed into the kitchen, rattling through drawers, the sound of glass clinking like warning bells. She sat stone-still, waiting for the next blow.

It came faster than she expected.

He returned, and without a word, struck her hard across the side of the head.

Her ear rang from the impact. The room lurched sideways.

She grabbed the edge of the couch to steady herself, blinking through the dizziness.

Later, in the bathroom, she would tilt her head and find the faint trail of blood that had pooled in her ear canal and trickled down her neck, hidden behind her hair. The red staining her fingertips as she wiped it away.

She said nothing.

She knew better.

That night, the house grew darker, quieter, as the air cooled and Steve drank himself into deeper oblivion. Sarah curled beneath the thin blanket on her makeshift bed in the downstairs corner, every muscle tight, bracing for what she knew would come.

It always did.

The footsteps came just past midnight.

Heavy. Clumsy. Reeking of whiskey.

She woke to the crushing weight of him pressing down on her, to the damp heat of his breath at her ear, to his hands fumbling at the hem of her shirt, sliding where they didn't belong.

"You're a *whore*, right?" he sneered, slurring the word like it tasted good. "Might as well get mine."

But this time—this time—something broke inside her.

She didn't thrash. Didn't scream. There was no point. He was over six feet tall, close to 300 pounds. She was barely a hundred, all skin and bone. She couldn't overpower him.

But she could face him.

She turned her head slowly, locked eyes with him. Her voice didn't shake. There were no tears.

Just steel.

"I can't stop you," she said through clenched teeth, her words sharp as glass. "But if you rape me, I will kill myself. And I will send a letter to the police to tell them why."

She held his gaze for a heartbeat longer. Then she looked away.

The silence that followed was heavier than his weight. His breath hitched. His grip faltered.

Slowly, he pulled back.

He rose unsteadily to his feet and stumbled down the hallway, disappearing into the bedroom he shared with her mother.

Sarah lay still beneath the blanket, her body trembling, but her eyes wide open. She didn't sleep. Not that night.

By morning, the house creaked with the weight of the unspoken.

Steve sat at the table nursing his coffee and his hangover. Hattie smoked her cigarette, her eyes vacant. Neither of them spoke of the night before. No one ever did.

But something had shifted.

Sarah wasn't told to sleep downstairs anymore.

She was given one of the upstairs bedrooms again.

It wasn't mercy.

It wasn't kindness.

It was fear.

Chapter 68

The air inside the farmhouse thickened after that night, dense and suffocating like humidity before a storm. Whatever thread had snapped between Sarah and Steve wasn't gone—it hung there, frayed and humming, ready to pull taut again. The tension seeped into the walls, into the floorboards, coiling beneath every creak and groan of the old house.

Steve avoided her now.

Not out of shame. Not out of guilt.

But out of calculation.

He didn't storm into her space unannounced anymore. His eyes no longer roamed when she crossed the room. He gave her a wide berth, but Sarah knew better than to believe it was respect. It was strategy. A man like Steve didn't back off unless he was planning something worse.

And Hattie...

Hattie changed too.

She still clung to her beer cans, still let her cigarette ash burn long and thin before flicking it away—but her silences were heavier now, weighted with something more than apathy. Her eyes, once dull and distant, tracked Steve differently. Warier. Like she'd seen something she couldn't unsee. Her hands trembled more often. Her hair had thinned. Her skin draped over her tiny frame.

Sarah didn't expect protection from her.

She never had.

But now, even the illusion of her mother's presence felt thinner.

When graduation neared, it was Randy who stepped up.

He and his wife, Katie, offered to buy Sarah a dress. No one else had even mentioned the ceremony. No one else cared. But Randy... Randy always showed up in those small, unexpected ways, patching over the broken parts where he could.

Katie was kind in a way that felt unfamiliar, soft but steady. She had weathered her own storms—a widow when she was twenty-three, raising a child on her own before finding Randy. Together they'd built a home that didn't reek of rot and regret. Their youngest, Jackson, four years old and all energy, had never known the kind of life Sarah had lived.

Randy had walked away from Steve's business long ago, cutting ties with the underworld that had claimed too many of their family. But he never cut ties with Mark or Sarah. He couldn't. He'd lived it too.

Sarah smiled and nodded as Katie held up dresses against her, weighing colors and cuts. But inside, she felt like she was trying on someone else's life. A girl with soft edges. A girl who belonged to a different story.

She wouldn't be wearing that dress to a new beginning.

Not yet.

She'd been accepted to colleges all over—doors out of Kentucky, out of the red clay and the rusted cars and the shadows that clung to her. But Steve? He slammed those doors shut.

"University of Louisville," he said flatly. "You can commute. No sense wasting money on dorms when you've got a roof over your head."

As if that roof wasn't a cage.

As if it wasn't control.

He didn't have to say it. She knew the real reason—he wanted her close. Close enough to keep her leashed, even as she pretended to leave.

During her senior year, he'd reluctantly allowed her to get a driver's license. But a license meant nothing without wheels. That freedom didn't come until the financial aid refund arrived—money meant for books and tuition, but just enough to buy a battered '76 Ford Maverick. Olive green, rust blooming along the edges, oil leaking like it was mourning its own life.

They paid in cash. Steve haggled the price down to nothing, grinning like he'd won something. Sarah watched the transaction through numb eyes, wondering if this was how escape felt—bitter, worn, and just out of reach.

He made her keep the leftover money in an envelope, tucked into the back of her dresser. "Track every penny," he told her, showing her how to log expenses in a ledger, neat columns of debits and credits. She followed the routine like a religion—gas, replacing oil that slowly leaked from the engine, changing spark plugs, an occasional sandwich between classes.

For a moment, she allowed herself to believe the lie.

That she was free.

That the car, the ledger, the life she was building could be hers.

But Steve was always watching.

It started small—a twenty here, a fifty there. He'd mutter something about borrowing. Paying it back. But she knew better. Every dollar fed his habit. Every missing bill was a needle in his vein.

Then came the wreck. His truck, mangled against a utility pole, left for dead on the side of a back road. After that, he took her Maverick like it was his own. Dropped her at campus with a greasy smile, promised to pick her up after class.

He always came back late.

Eyes glassy, breath sharp with stale liquor, reeking of tobacco and something darker—like sweat, rage, and sleepless nights.

And still, she said nothing.

Because what could she say?

What could she do?

That car, that ledger, that fragile thread of independence—they were never hers.

Not really.

Just another leash.

Just another chain.

And the weight of it settled in her bones.

Chapter 69

The sickness hit her like a brick wall—sudden, sharp, and unforgiving.

One moment, Sarah sat in her morning class, pen poised over her notebook, the lecture droning on about cell structures and DNA. The next, a wave of nausea surged through her like a riptide, dragging her from the edges of consciousness. She bolted upright, her heart pounding, vision tilting, and stumbled from her seat before the teacher could finish the sentence.

The hallway swayed around her, walls bending as her knees buckled beneath her. She made it to the nearest restroom, flinging herself into the stall just in time to retch violently, her body convulsing with each heave. Bile burned her throat. Her arms shook as she clung to the toilet bowl, her cheek pressing to the cold tile floor. The coolness grounded her for a moment—just long enough to stop the spinning.

But the pain didn't let go.

A deep, gnawing ache radiated from her side, pulsing sharper with every breath. She dragged herself upright, rinsed her mouth at the sink, and stared into the mirror. Her reflection startled her—pale skin waxy, eyes glassy and sunken, strands of sweat-matted hair clinging to her forehead.

The student health clinic wasn't far, but each step there felt like climbing a mountain. Her limbs dragged behind her like dead weight. When she finally slumped into the nurse's chair, the woman took one glance at Sarah's face, her hunched posture, the sheen of sweat, and nodded knowingly.

"Virus going around," the nurse said, too dismissive, too practiced. She handed Sarah a chalky Phenergan tablet and a paper cup of lukewarm water, as if that would cure whatever was unraveling beneath her ribs.

Sarah swallowed it down without a word.

There was nowhere else to go. No bed to crawl into. No phone to call home. She wandered to a far corner of the new student center—a place barely finished, the walls still smelling faintly of fresh paint. She found an old burgundy bench tucked near a drafty window. It wasn't soft. It wasn't warm. But it was somewhere to be small.

She curled up, arms wrapped around her aching side, head pressed to the cold glass, eyes fluttering shut. She couldn't let herself sleep, not too long. She couldn't miss Steve. He'd be waiting at McDonald's at 3 o'clock sharp. There'd be no forgiveness if she was late.

By two, she peeled herself off the bench. The nausea crept back like a wave rising behind her. Halfway across campus, it knocked her off her feet again. She arrived at McDonalds just in time to duck into another restroom, retching until there was nothing left but the ache in her ribs and the salt on her lips. She leaned against the stall wall, her breath shallow, chest rising and falling like a trapped bird.

At three, she sat on the curb outside McDonald's, arms folded tight across her stomach, rocking slightly as she waited. The sky blurred, the heat of the asphalt pressing against her through her jeans.

The sputter of her Maverick rattled up the street.

Steve behind the wheel. Glassy-eyed. Silent.

He didn't ask how she felt. He didn't care. The car smelled like oil and smoke, like Steve's addiction seeping from the upholstery.

Home.

Hattie met them at the door, her eyes scanning Sarah's pale face with something close to concern. Without a word, she guided Sarah into the bed by the window—the same bed where Sarah had once curled beneath the thin quilt, bracing against the sound of footsteps in the night.

This time, Sarah barely protested. She lay down, her body too hollow, too broken to resist.

Steve didn't linger. He dropped her off like a parcel and vanished to the river bottoms—seeking comfort at the bottom of a bottle before the Dilaudid high faded while Sarah twisted in pain.

By nightfall, Sarah was in agony.

Sweat soaked her hair, the sheets damp beneath her. Every breath felt sharp, stabbing at her ribs. Her abdomen pulsed with fire, the pain spreading wider, deeper.

Hattie hovered.

She pressed her hand against Sarah's belly, felt the heat, the tightness beneath the skin. As she released, Sarah cried out in pain. Hattie's lips thinned, cigarette clinging to the corner of her mouth. She'd seen this before. She knew.

Appendix.

Maybe ruptured.

But the house had no phone. The bill had been unpaid for months. The only option was the landlord—Jack and Ruby—five hundred yards away, through the dark.

Hattie pulled on her jacket, the sleeves too loose, the shoulders slumped. She walked through the night, cigarette smoke trailing behind her like a ghost, shoes crunching the gravel. She knocked. Used the phone. Called around.

No one could find Steve.

She returned, slower, shoulders sagging beneath the weight of too many bad choices. She sat beside Sarah's bed and waited.

Midnight.

The door creaked open, bringing the sour reek of whiskey and sweat. Steve stumbled through, slamming the door behind him, muttering curses into the dark.

Hattie stood.

"We're taking her to the hospital."

Steve sneered, glancing toward Sarah's curled frame.

"She's fakin'," he muttered, swaying in the doorway. "She'll be fine."

Hattie didn't back down.

The ride to the hospital was a blur of curses and accusations. Steve barked at Hattie, grumbled about Sarah's dramatics. Every bump in the road sent knives through her abdomen, each jolt a fresh wave of agony.

But when the triage nurse saw her, everything changed.

Within minutes, Sarah was rushed behind double doors—wheeled down sterile hallways, past the cold glow of machines. The CT scan confirmed what Hattie already knew.

Ruptured appendix.

Emergency surgery.

Sarah faded in and out beneath the fluorescent lights, her body trembling uncontrollably. Somewhere nearby, she heard Steve's voice break in a way she hadn't before.

"I'm sorry," he stammered. "I didn't know. I love you."

But Sarah didn't believe him.

The gurney rolled away from him, the hum of machines swallowing his words.

And then—

Darkness.

When she woke, the world was soft and still. A slow beep from the monitor. The faint rustle of a nurse's shoes. Hattie slumped in the corner recliner, purse still clutched in her lap, eyes closed.

Steve hovered at the door later that morning. A shadow. He

muttered something about being sorry. About it never happening again.

Then he was gone.

Hattie followed shortly after, mumbling something about heading home for a beer.

Sarah didn't mind.

The room was quiet. Safe. For two days, she lay beneath crisp white sheets, visited by nurses with kind hands and soft smiles. Nuns in long habits stopped by, offering prayers. She let them. Maybe their words could reach where hers couldn't.

When it was time to leave, she barely looked back.

At home, the silence resumed. No one asked how she felt. No one offered help.

By the end of the week, it was as if nothing had ever happened.

Chapter 70

For a brief sliver of time after Sarah returned home from the hospital, the house grew quieter. Steve's temper dulled, his voice lowered, and the sharp edges of their world softened just enough to breathe. It was like the threat of losing control had forced him, if only for a moment, to remember his own humanity.

But it never lasted.

Not with him.

The old patterns crept back in like weeds breaking through cracked pavement. The money dried up—same as always. His cravings gnawed at the edges of his control, twisting him back into something jagged and mean. But the Dilaudid was out of reach now—too expensive, too scarce.

So he returned to the bottle.

But not the whiskey.

This time, it was MD 20/20. Cheap, syrupy wine that stained his lips a deep, bruised purple and smelled like rotten fruit fermenting in the sun. He called it "mad dog" with a grin, like it made him dangerous, like it made him proud. One bottle. Then another. Then more. The money from Hattie's dwindling Social Security check stretched thin— barely enough for groceries, let alone Steve's insatiable thirst.

He didn't work. Claimed no one would hire him. Claimed he was "too smart for that kind of shit anyway." But the truth was simpler:

work meant someone telling him what to do, holding him accountable. Steve didn't answer to anyone. Never had.

So he drank.

And when he drank, the poison inside him rose to the surface. His bitterness festered, his resentment soured the air. It soaked into the walls, into Sarah's skin like something she couldn't wash off.

One night, the television flickered in the corner—Country Music Awards flashing on the screen, golden lights and big hats, laughter from a world far away. Hattie sat slouched in the recliner, chain-smoking, her beer sweating on the table. Steve sprawled in his chair, his belly hanging heavy, the mad dog bottle balanced precariously between his knees.

Sarah moved through the living room like a ghost—silent, invisible. But Steve's eyes caught her, tracking her like prey.

"Hey."

The word snapped the air, too casual to trust.

Sarah stopped mid-step, her arms hanging at her sides, her stomach curling.

"You ever drink before?" His words slurred at the edges but held that dangerous lilt. The bait. He knew the answer.

Sarah's throat tightened. She turned slowly, her face neutral, but her heart pounding.

"No," she said softly. "I don't want to."

For a moment, silence.

Then Steve's mouth twisted—not into a smile, but something darker.

"Think you're better than me, huh?" His voice rose, just enough to sour the room. The kind of rise that meant there was no right answer.

She shook her head quickly. "No. I just... I don't like it."

He laughed, sharp and mean—a sound that made Hattie glance up but not speak. The flame from her lighter flickered as she lit another cigarette, eyes drifting back to the table, back to nowhere.

"Well," Steve said, pushing up from the couch, towering over Sarah with the bottle clutched in one hand, "we're gonna change that."

The bottle sloshed as he shoved it toward her, the neon liquid catching the light like something radioactive.

"Drink. All of it."

Sarah's pulse thundered in her ears. The smell hit her first—sweet and rancid, like melted candy left too long in the sun. Her fingers trembled as she took the bottle, cold glass biting into her palms.

She raised it to her lips.

The first sip burned like acid.

The second burned worse.

The sweetness coated her tongue like syrup gone bad, making her gag. But she drank it. Every drop.

Because not drinking it meant something worse.

Steve watched her the whole time, his lips curling into a slow, satisfied grin.

"Good girl," he muttered, sinking back into his seat with a grunt, his eyes glazed, his belly rising and falling like a beast at rest.

Sarah sat there, swaying slightly, the room tilting beneath her feet. Her stomach roiled. Her throat clenched. She glanced toward Hattie, hoping for a flicker of something—concern, regret. But Hattie just dragged on her cigarette, her face gray in the television's glow.

At the first chance, Sarah turned and climbed the narrow stairs. Her legs felt unsteady beneath her, her head thick and heavy. The taste of mad dog clung to the back of her throat like tar.

She reached her room, and collapsed onto the thin mattress. Curled into herself. The spinning came fast—the world tilting, her stomach heaving.

She closed her eyes and willed herself not to cry.

Because this—this wasn't just about drinking. This was about power. About reminding her who held the leash.

As the room spun and the bile crept up her throat, Sarah held onto the only thing she could—the dream that one day, none of this would touch her again.

She let the sickness take her under.

At least in sleep, there was escape.

Chapter 71

The house was still when Sarah got home that afternoon, its sagging frame silhouetted against a sky smeared in grays and soft golds. The late summer heat clung to the walls, the air thick with the lingering scent of damp earth and cigarette smoke. Steve and Hattie were gone— off to the river bottoms or maybe some backroad bar where the beer was cheap and nobody cared how many skeletons followed you in.

The silence was uneasy, like a hollow shell left behind after something dangerous slithered out.

Sarah took what peace she could. She swept the kitchen floor, wiped down the counters, started dinner from scraps. Canned beans. Instant potatoes. A pack of freezer-burned ground beef. It wasn't much, but it was enough to fill a plate. Enough to give the illusion of a meal.

She was eighteen now. Legal. An adult in the eyes of the world. But in that house? She was still a prisoner. Every day she weighed her options—measured escape against the weight of fear, the thickness of the unknown.

Until that night.

The sun had long dipped beneath the hills when Steve and Hattie stumbled through the door. The smell of beer and sweat hit the walls like a storm. Steve's boots scuffed across the linoleum, his voice already rising, laughter sharp and mean. Hattie lagged behind, her head bobbing, a cigarette burned down to the filter between her fingers.

Sarah finished cooking in silence, scraping the last bits from the pan, cleaning the dishes before they could find fault with her. She moved quietly, like a shadow. Like always.

She settled at the coffee table with her textbooks, the familiar act of pretending to focus, the scratch of her pencil steady even as the tension thickened behind her.

Hattie's head drooped in her chair, her beer tipped precariously. Steve's eyes locked on her, the shift in his body subtle but sharp.

"Wake up, you drunk bitch," he snapped, his words slurred but still edged like broken glass.

Hattie mumbled something—a soft, slurry protest.

That was all it took.

Steve rose from his chair in three slow, deliberate strides, stood over her, and slapped the sides of her head—once, twice, sharp cracks that echoed in the stale air. Hattie jolted, blinking slowly, bringing her hands up to shield her face, but didn't fight back. She never did.

Then, as quickly as it started, he dropped back into his chair, sinking into the sagging cushion, the room silent again.

Sarah didn't move. Her pencil hovered mid-word. The scratch of graphite had stopped, but her heart thundered loud enough to drown out thought.

Hattie wobbled to her feet, muttered something about needing another beer, and stumbled toward the kitchen.

When she returned, cold can in hand, Steve's eyes followed her. A low growl rumbled from his chest.

Without warning, he lunged.

Hattie barely had time to brace before he grabbed her, dragging her down from the chair, slamming her onto the floor. The beer can clattered away, rolling beneath the table. His fists came next. Heavy, blunt, relentless. Kicks drove into her ribs. The thud of bone on wood.

Her body curled into itself, a futile shield.

Sarah sat frozen, her back pressed into the sofa, the air clawing at her throat. She didn't move. Didn't dare.

When Steve was done, he hauled Hattie back up and tossed her into the chair like a rag doll. Blood traced the corner of her mouth, her eyes glassy, half-closed. She swayed slightly, a marionette with cut strings.

Then Steve turned.

His eyes locked on Sarah—bloodshot, full of something wild and rotting.

"I should've killed her while I had her down there," he spat, venom thick on his tongue.

Sarah's breath caught in her chest. Something shifted inside her— something small, but solid. The last thread of tolerance snapped, soundless but final.

Steve stared at her too long, reading the change on her face.

He turned, lumbered down the hallway, and disappeared into the bedroom. But not before, snatching her car keys from the hook by the door and dropping them onto the nightstand beside him—close enough to see, far enough to taunt.

A warning. A leash.

Sarah waited.

She counted the minutes. The muffled curses from the bedroom. The groan of the bed frame. The thud of boots kicked off onto the floor.

When the house grew still—when the night swallowed the last drunken mutters—she moved.

Upstairs. Quiet. Silent as breath. She sat in the dark on the side of her bed, listening for the creaks in the floorboards to settle, for the guttural snores to rumble from the back room.

One hour.

Then two.

She slipped on her shoes, stuffed her ID and crumpled the last handful of dollars into her pocket. It wasn't much—just enough to get somewhere, anywhere.

She crept down the stairs, every step measured, toes pressed into the soft spots between the boards. Past the living room, where beer cans lay scattered like forgotten promises. Past the doorway to the bedroom.

She paused there.

The keys glinted on the nightstand.

But she didn't take them.

She wouldn't risk the sound, wouldn't risk waking him. Not tonight.

Instead, she eased open the side door, slipped out into the humid dark, and pulled it closed behind her with a soft click.

The night air was heavy, thick with the song of crickets and cicadas, the sky a sea of stars overhead. The dirt of the driveway stirred with every step.

She walked.

The highway ran directly in front of the old farmhouse. She took off toward the right and headed toward Bardstown.. Two miles east, the glow of a convenience store flickered faintly in the distance.

Every time headlights approached, she dove into the weeds, heart pounding, breath held tight in her chest.

She didn't have a plan.

Just the will to keep moving.

Because tonight, she was leaving.

Even if it was only for a night—

She was free.

Chapter 72

The convenience store loomed quiet and lifeless, its flickering fluorescent sign stuttering against the dark sky like a dying heartbeat. Sarah stood at the edge of the parking lot, her body pressed into the shadows, watching the pool of pale light that spilled across the cracked asphalt. The hum of passing traffic whispered from the highway, engines grumbling through the night, but here—beneath that sputtering glow—everything felt still. Empty.

The pay phone stood mounted against the side of the building, cold metal shining under the buzzing light. Sarah stepped toward it, her heart hammering as if she were running, though her feet moved slow and cautious. She picked up the receiver, hands trembling, and dialed zero. The operator's voice felt too loud in the silence.

"Collect call from Sarah," the robotic voice echoed.

Janet accepted.

Janet had always been around, floating at the edges of her mother's life like smoke—less a friend, more a drinking buddy with a streak of kindness that surfaced when it mattered most. Sarah's words came clipped and hurried. Enough to explain, enough to plead. No details. Just *come.*

The receiver clicked down, the connection gone, and she was left standing beneath the flickering sign, counting her heartbeat in the dark.

Fifteen minutes passed. Then thirty.

Every set of headlights that rounded the bend sent her heart leaping into her throat. She crouched low behind the vending machines each time, breath tight in her chest, the gravel biting into her palms as she watched from the shadows.

She imagined the roar of Steve's truck. The glare of his headlights finding her like prey. She pictured him storming from the cab, the way his hands curled into fists before the blow ever landed. She could almost smell the whiskey on his breath.

But it wasn't Steve.

A familiar sedan rolled slow into the lot, headlights dimmed, the engine idling low. Sarah stepped forward cautiously, heart pounding in her ears.

Janet leaned across the seat, the cherry of her cigarette glowing faint in the dark.

"Get in, baby," she murmured, voice soft but sure.

Sarah slipped into the passenger seat, the door closing with a gentle *click* that sounded too loud in the quiet. Neither of them spoke. Janet didn't ask. She didn't have to. She just turned the wheel and pulled back onto the highway, her eyes fixed forward, smoke curling lazily from her lips.

At Janet's apartment in Loretto—a cramped second-floor unit above a laundromat—the scent of fabric softener clung to the air. Sarah curled onto the couch without untying her shoes, the thin blanket scratchy against her skin. Sleep came in fits, her body stiff, her mind wired for danger.

But morning brought clarity.

She couldn't go back.

Not this time.

When Janet returned from the kitchen, mug of coffee in hand, Sarah sat up, rubbing the knot at the base of her skull.

"I need to go to the police," she said softly, the words tasting foreign in her mouth.

Janet didn't blink. She nodded once, slow and sure, and set the mug down.

The drive to the station felt longer than it was, the weight of the decision pressing down with every passing mile. Inside, the station smelled of old coffee and disinfectant. Sarah sat across from a tired-looking officer, his badge worn, his eyes lined with the kind of exhaustion that never quite leaves.

She told him everything.

Steve's violence. The blows. The threats. How he had towered over Hattie, spit flying from his mouth as he roared that he should've killed her when he had the chance.

She told them about the weapons—borrowed guns, a shotgun and rifle tucked away in the house.

She didn't tell them everything. Not about the drugs. Not about the cellar greenhouse, the past crimes that could've buried him. She wasn't trying to ruin him.

She just wanted him gone.

So she could get her mother out.

For all Hattie's failures—her silences, her complicity—she was still *Mom.* That had to count for something.

The officer nodded, jotting notes, his pen scratching slowly across the paper.

"Go wait at that gas station," he instructed. "We'll take care of it. You wait for an officer to come back to tell you when it's clear."

Janet and Sarah returned to the edge of the same parking lot, parking near the tree line where the morning sun sliced through the branches in thin golden beams. Janet smoked quietly, her gaze fixed on the horizon, while Sarah sat rigid, every muscle tight as a wire.

Then came the cruisers.

Five in all, lights spinning in silence, engines roaring as they disappeared down the road.

It was happening.

Nearly an hour passed. The weight of it stretched long, each minute twisting tighter. Finally, one cruiser returned, dust rising behind it. The officer stepped out, his posture casual, but his eyes sharp.

"It's done," he said simply. "He's out. Weapons confiscated. He can't come back for twenty-four hours. You can go back now... if you still want her."

Sarah's throat closed. She nodded once.

They followed the cruiser back to the farmhouse, gravel crunching under the tires, the sky wide and pale above.

Sarah stepped out slowly, the air thick with something heavier than dread. She pushed open the front door, her heart skittering like a trapped thing.

Hattie stood in the center of the living room, eyes rimmed red, mouth twisted with betrayal.

"What the hell did you do?" she spat, voice low and sharp. "Why would you *do* this?"

Sarah didn't answer.

Didn't flinch.

She turned, climbed the stairs, and packed. Her hands moved steady, gathering what little she owned. A few shirts. A threadbare hoodie. Her school books, worn at the edges.

Downstairs, Janet tried to reason with Hattie, her voice muffled beneath the hum of the kitchen fan.

When Sarah returned, duffel bag slung over her shoulder, Hattie stood there, arms crossed, a storm behind her eyes. For a moment, neither spoke.

Then, without warning, Hattie stepped forward and wrapped her arms around Sarah.

Tight. Desperate.

"Thank you," she whispered, her voice raw.

And in that moment, something shifted.

The storm cracked.

And for the first time in a long time, Sarah felt something close to hope.

Chapter 73

Janet turned to Hattie, her voice flat and unyielding.

"Pack a bag," she ordered. "We're not staying here long."

The words landed hard. The police might've removed Steve from the house, might've confiscated his guns, but Sarah knew what a restraining order really meant. Paper. Not protection. It couldn't stop him from circling back like a buzzard, waiting for them to let their guard down.

Janet had seen this too many times. She wasn't about to wait for the knock on the door.

The weight of what Sarah had done still clung to her skin like sweat when they pulled into Janet's apartment lot. Gravel crackled beneath the tires, the faint hum of distant traffic humming through the open window. Janet parked close to the door, her eyes sweeping the lot before cutting the engine. The night before had been a blur, but this-this was when the fear settled into Sarah's bones.

The hours dragged inside that small apartment. The television flickered with reruns no one watched. Cigarette smoke curled and clung to the faded wallpaper, thickening the air as Hattie sat hunched on the couch, the cordless phone perched in her lap like a lifeline that wouldn't hold.

Her hands trembled as she punched in the numbers, redialing the same handful of people over and over, each call another crack in the dam.

First, Randy.

"No, Mom," came his voice, clipped and final. "I've got my own family now. I can't risk that kind of trouble near my kids...I'm sorry."

Click.

Next, Vanessa.

"I'm sorry," she whispered. "I just... I can't. Not with my boys. Not again."

Mark was unreachable—thousands of miles away in Hawaii, drowning in his own battles, his voice too distant even if she could have reached him.

Hattie's face crumpled a little more with each call.

Finally, she dialed Diane.

There was no hesitation on the other end.

"Come on," Diane said. "You can stay here till you figure things out. But you need to be done this time."

By dusk, Janet's car rolled into Diane's driveway, headlights sweeping across the patchy lawn, illuminating the modest split-level house like a lighthouse in the dark. The porch light glowed steady, casting long shadows across the steps. Diane stood waiting at the door, cigarette dangling between two fingers, her other hand gripping a dish towel like it was the only thing anchoring her to patience.

"Get in here," she snapped, waving them inside before the engine had even cooled.

Inside, the house smelled like coffee and fried chicken, the sharp tang of cigarette smoke barely masking the warmth beneath. Diane led Sarah down the hallway, her voice softening as she pushed open the door to a small, neat bedroom.

"You'll stay in Leslie's room," she said. "She moved out a few months ago. You make yourself at home, honey."

The bedspread was pale blue, patterned with delicate flowers. The walls held framed pictures-Leslie as a child, smiling wide, arms around her mother. The whole room felt foreign, like it belonged to a different world.

Sarah didn't unpack. She dropped her bag by the dresser and collapsed onto the bed, her body sinking into the soft mattress as though it might swallow her whole. The moment her head touched the pillow, the weight of the last few days bore down, dragging her into a deep, heavy sleep.

It was the first time she had slept without fear of footsteps in the hall.

When she woke, the sky outside had dimmed to that soft blue—gray of early evening, the kind of light that blurred the edges of everything. She padded quietly down the hall, following the faint murmur of voices to the kitchen.

Diane's voice cut sharp through the soft clatter of dishes.

"I'm telling you, Hattie—if you even *think* about going back to that bastard, I'm done."

Sarah froze in the doorway, her breath caught in her throat.

"I won't have him near my house," Diane continued, her voice low but fierce. "If you go back to him, you're on your own. You won't drag this mess into my life unless you're serious about getting out this time."

"He called," Hattie whispered, her voice fraying at the edges. "He found us. Said it was Sarah's fault. Said she cost him everything-his money, his plants..."

Diane snorted, loud and bitter.

"Good. Let it rot," she snapped. "You think I give a damn about his drug money? He's lucky she didn't tell them *everything*. He's lucky they didn't haul him straight to prison."

Hattie's voice wavered. "He says he still loves me."

Diane slammed her coffee mug down hard enough to rattle the

table.

"He doesn't love you. He *owns* you. There's a difference."

A silence settled between them, thick as tar. Then Diane added, her voice softer but no less fierce, "He threatened *me*, Hattie. Said me and Rich were keeping 'his woman' from him. You want to go back to that?"

Sarah couldn't listen anymore.

She turned away, slipping back down the hall, her stomach churning with dread. She knew this pattern too well-the pull, the promise, the slow slide back into hell.

But Diane wasn't like the others. Diane was steel.

Rich, too, had a quiet steadiness, sitting in his recliner like a man who'd seen too much to be rattled now. And their son, Chad, back from college for the weekend, was like a mountain carved from flesh and bone-six-foot-ten, three hundred pounds, all muscle and calm.

When Chad spotted Sarah hovering near the hallway, pale and wide-eyed, he gave her a soft smile that didn't match the bulk of him.

"Hey," he said gently, his voice low and warm. "Don't worry. You're safe here. Nothing's gonna happen to you while I'm around."

Sarah blinked, the kindness in his voice cutting sharper than any cruelty.

And for the first time in what felt like forever, she almost believed it.

Chapter 74

It only took a few days.

A handful of tense, whispered phone calls. The weight of history pressing down on decisions that should have been easy but never were.

And just like that—Hattie made her choice.

She was going back.

Diane had warned her from the start. Made it clear in the sharp, no-nonsense way that only Diane could.

"If you leave," she said, cigarette burning low between her fingers, "you don't come back."

But it didn't stop her.

Sarah knew it wouldn't.

When Steve's car crept up Diane's driveway, its headlights dull in the gray afternoon, it didn't just idle—it loomed. The engine rumbled like a threat beneath its rusted hood, the windows tinted dark enough to hide the man inside. But Sarah didn't need to see him. She felt his presence from behind the blinds where she stood, her heart pounding like fists on a locked door.

Chad was already outside, filling the porch with his six-foot-ten frame of muscle as a silent warning. Arms crossed, jaw set. He stood like a wall that wouldn't be moved.

Steve didn't get out.

He didn't have to.

He sat behind the wheel, one hand lazily tapping the steering column, the other probably wrapped around the neck of a beer bottle or something worse. The engine idled low, vibrating through the ground, as if daring anyone to challenge him.

Hattie moved quietly through Diane's house—barely there, gathering her small bag with the practiced hands of someone who'd done this dance too many times before. She clutched a fresh twelve-pack of beer under her arm like a ticket home.

She paused only long enough to give Sarah a quick hug—if you could call it that. It felt more like an afterthought. Limp arms. A mumbled string of words that dissolved before they hit the air. Maybe a goodbye. Maybe not.

She didn't look back.

Sarah stood frozen at the window, the blinds cool beneath her fingertips, and watched her mother cross the threshold, walk the gravel drive, and slide into the passenger seat. The door slammed shut, the engine growled to life, and the car backed down the driveway, disappearing into the haze of the late afternoon.

Gone.

The door closed behind them with a weight Sarah felt in her bones.

Diane found her still standing in the hall, arms folded tightly across her chest like she could hold herself together if she just pressed hard enough.

"You can stay here," Diane said, voice soft but lined with steel. "As long as you're in school. But your mom?" She shook her head once. "She's made her choice. She's not walking back through that door."

Sarah nodded, swallowing down the ache that rose in her throat. Scared that without her being there to share the abuse, she may have just said goodbye to her mother forever.

Three days passed in a fragile, uneasy rhythm. School. Homework.

The occasional quiet dinner with Diane and Rich, their home steady and solid in a way Sarah had never known. For the first time in what felt like forever, there was space to breathe.

Then the phone rang.

Sarah sat in the next room, every muscle coiled as she listened to Diane's voice rise and fall in the kitchen. At first, it was calm, measured. Then it snapped, sharp as a breaking branch.

"No, Hattie. No, you don't get to do this."

A pause.

"I told you what would happen."

Another pause.

The receiver slammed down, rattling the table.

Diane came into the room, her face carved with weariness. She looked at Sarah like she wanted to offer something—comfort, maybe—but the truth hung too heavy between them.

Sarah didn't ask what her mother had said.

She already knew.

And just when the ground beneath her feet began to steady, just when she thought maybe—just maybe—she could exhale, the world tilted again.

Steve had gone on one of his "business trips," this time to Paducah. But he didn't come back the same.

The call came while he was still on the road. His voice was raw, no pretense of charm or lies.

"Pack your shit and get out before I get home," he barked at Hattie. "I've got someone else now."

Her name was Julie. A new woman. A fresh start for him. Another dead end for Hattie.

With nowhere else to go, Hattie picked up the phone again.

And against every line she'd drawn, every rule she'd laid down, Diane agreed to take her back in—but only for a week.

Just long enough to figure something out.

Sarah said nothing. She didn't trust her voice to hold.

Instead, she picked up more shifts at the hotel—scrubbing floors, making beds, pushing the cart down long, dim hallways, stretching every dollar she could. It wasn't much, but it was something. Enough to scrape by. Enough to survive.

Within a few days, they found a small one-bedroom apartment on the south end of town. The kind of place that smelled like old paint and echoes. The rent was barely manageable, the walls thin enough to hear the neighbors' television at night.

But it was theirs.

They moved in with almost nothing.

A battered couch donated by a friend. A dining table with one leg braced by a stack of National Geographics. Two mismatched chairs. A twin bed they took turns sleeping on. A coffee table that

It wasn't much.

But it was quiet.

No shouting. No footsteps in the hallway. No door slamming at two a.m. No Steve.

For the first time in years, Sarah let herself breathe.

It wasn't home.

But it was safe.

Chapter 75

The feeling of safety didn't last long.

Barely a month had passed since settling into the tiny apartment with Hattie. The walls were still bare, the furniture sparse, but it had felt like enough—a fragile cocoon of quiet.

Then Sarah turned the corner in the back hallway of the hotel, where the housekeepers clocked in and stored their carts—and froze.

Evan.

And Julie.

Standing together in the laundry room like they belonged there. Like they hadn't just dragged her entire world back into the dark.

It was as if someone had ripped the stitches from a half-healed wound. Sarah stood there, pulse pounding in her ears, the hum of industrial dryers suddenly deafening. She could barely move.

Steve had sent them.

She knew it without question.

They didn't need the jobs. Not really. Not there. This wasn't about money—it was about Steve reminding her she couldn't outrun him. He wanted her trapped, cornered. Always looking over her shoulder.

The hotel's fluorescent lights buzzed overhead, flickering just enough to make the shadows shift, stretching long down the corridor. Sarah felt the weight of it settle back onto her chest.

Julie claimed the laundry room, stationed at the counter folding towels, her fake smile pinned on like a mask. Evan floated freely—a houseman—retrieving dirty linens, delivering clean ones to the carts. His role gave him permission to move through the halls, past her, behind her. Close enough to whisper, close enough to remind her she wasn't safe.

At first, he didn't bother with subtlety.

"Where you living now?" he asked one morning, feigning casual interest as he dumped a heap of sheets onto her cart.

Sarah didn't look up.

Didn't answer.

The next day, it was:

"Traffic bad today? You coming in from far?"

Then:

"Still staying over on the south end?"

Each question wrapped in something soft, like they weren't meant to cut. But Sarah felt every edge.

She gave him nothing.

The routine settled like a noose. Every afternoon when her shift ended, she clocked out quickly—but the lot outside felt like a trap. Steve circled. Always circling. Sometimes parked with the engine idling, sometimes leaning back against the truck like he had all the time in the world.

Sarah learned to wait. She hid in the stairwell behind the second-floor landing, sitting low against the wall, listening for the grumble of the truck engine, waiting for the vultures to fly off. Sometimes minutes passed. Sometimes hours. She listened for the click of Julie's shoes, the careless scuff of Evan's sneakers, and the roar of tires pulling away.

Only then would she slip out.

But even the exits came with risk.

One afternoon, luck was on her side. She finished early and bolted for the door. The lot was empty. She sprinted to her car—the old green Maverick that clattered and coughed but was hers.

As she turned onto the road, the world narrowed.

Steve's truck barreled toward her, swerving across the yellow line.

Sarah jerked the wheel, tires screeching as she veered onto the shoulder. Gravel spit from beneath her tires as he passed within inches, his truck grazing the air beside her like a hand brushing too close.

A message.

A warning.

You can't escape.

Her knuckles whitened on the steering wheel, her breath shallow as she waited for the shaking to subside.

But then, after months of torment—like the wind—they were gone.

Evan. Julie. Steve's truck. All of them.

No warnings. No goodbyes.

Just silence.

But Sarah didn't relax. She couldn't. She kept her routines unpredictable—never parking in the same spot twice, watching over her shoulder, memorizing every face in the lot.

It became second nature. Hypervigilance stitched into her bones.

Still, as the days stretched without their shadows, something loosened in her chest. A tether frayed.

Weeks passed. Then a month.

The tension began to uncoil.

One evening after her shift, Sarah stood by the apartment window, peeling back the curtain just enough to peer out. The streetlamp buzzed in the distance, casting gold-tinted halos on the sidewalk. The night was quiet, still.

No headlights.

No truck.

No Steve.

The world outside blurred through the breath that fogged the glass.

And inside—behind the pane, behind the paper-thin walls—Sarah exhaled.

For the first time in years, she wasn't hunted.

The silence wasn't waiting to snap closed like a trap. It just was. Calm. Steady.

Safe.

She pressed her forehead to the window, the cool glass grounding her, and let the quiet wash over her.

She was still here.

She had made it through.

And in the stillness of that small apartment, Sarah allowed herself to believe the impossible.

Freedom.

It was fragile. It was uncertain.

But it was hers.

Epilogue

There was no parade. No crowd of witnesses. No sweeping music to mark the moment she slipped free. Just quiet.

For Sarah, freedom didn't arrive like a storm—it came in fragments. In the hush of a morning where no voices were raised. In the gentle click of a key turning in a lock that opened to *her* place—an apartment with thin walls and peeling paint, but peace folded into every corner. It came in the rhythm of paychecks earned on her own terms. In standing upright without apology. In knowing that every meal in the fridge, every clean sheet, every lamp left on at night came from her own two hands.

It came in *stillness.*

In nights without holding her breath. In mornings where the only sound was the hum of traffic outside and the laughter of her children, not the crack of fists on doors or the low growl of danger breathing down the hallway.

Freedom wasn't loud. It was steady.

But the past never vanished.

It lingered in the mirror on bad days, in the sharp edge of certain memories that hadn't yet dulled. It whispered sometimes, curling beneath the ribs when she least expected it. And on rare nights, it howled. But it no longer ruled her. It no longer dictated who she was allowed to become.

There were scars, of course. Some were visible—thin white lines along her arms, the way her hands sometimes trembled when things got too loud. But most lived in silence: the instinct to flinch, the way she checked door locks twice, the way she scanned every room for exits without even realizing it.

Still—she had made it out.

And that was everything.

She built a life—not perfect, not untouched by pain—but *hers.* A life where the floor didn't creak beneath angry footsteps. Where the clink of keys didn't mean danger. Where supper was filled with laughter, and bedtime stories were never interrupted by slammed doors.

She raised daughters who never had to hide under tables or tiptoe through the day. Daughters who knew what love looked like because she gave it to them without fear. And years later, she would hold grandsons in her arms—bright, wild boys with soft eyes and loud laughs—and know in her bones that the cycle had shattered.

She had broken it.

The girl who once curled into corners now stood in sunlight.

She had taken back her story.

She had spoken the truth out loud.

And for the girl in the window—for the barefoot child who once watched the world from behind a pane of glass, unseen and unheard— that was enough.

That was *everything.*

Afterword

This story was not easy to tell. It took over twenty years to write—because there were memories I wasn't ready to face, truths I wasn't ready to name. There were seasons I had to put it away entirely, shut the pages, and pretend it could wait. But silence has a weight of its own. And I carried that weight for too long.

Writing this book was not just an act of remembrance—it was an act of survival. Of reclamation. Of truth.

To those who have endured trauma, who have been silenced or shamed or made to feel small: I see you. Your pain is real, and your story matters. You are not alone. And you are not what happened to you.

To the people who showed me kindness when I needed it most—whether for a night, a season, or a lifetime—thank you. Your presence may have been brief, but your impact was lasting.

To my siblings, my younger self, and the children we once were: I carried you with me through every chapter. You deserved better. And through these pages, I hope you find the validation and voice we were denied for so long.

And to the reader who made it to the end—thank you. Thank you for witnessing. Thank you for staying. Thank you for holding space for this journey.

This story doesn't end with escape. Or healing. Or even peace. It continues—through choices made daily, through boundaries set, through generations that will grow up free.

And that, perhaps, is the greatest victory of all.

—S. Lee Davis

About the Author

S. Lee Davis grew up in rural Kentucky, where the events of *The Girl in the Window* took place. A survivor of generational trauma, she spent over two decades finding the strength—and the words—to tell her story.

Now a healthcare professional, Davis has dedicated her life to caring for and protecting others. She is the proud mother of two daughters and grandmother to two beautiful grandsons. She lives in Louisville, Kentucky.

Since writing her memoir, Davis has begun working on a series of psychological thrillers that explore survival, silence, and the secrets we carry. *The Girl in the Window* is her first book.

www.ingramcontent.com/pod-product-compliance
Lightning Source LLC
Chambersburg PA
CBHW021609120626
46545CB00001B/147